DEVON

– IN THE –

GREAT WAR

1914–1918

Gerald Wasley

DEVON BOOKS

First published in Great Britain by Devon Books in 2000

British Library Cataloguing-in-Publication Data
A CIP record for this title is available from the British Library

ISBN 1 85522 742 8

DEVON BOOKS
Official Publisher to Devon County Council

Halsgrove House
Lower Moor Way
Tiverton, Devon EX16 6SS
Tel: 01884 243242
Fax: 01884 243325
website: www.halsgrove.com

DEDICATION

For Sylvia Mary

Printed and bound by Bookcraft, Midsomer Norton

CONTENTS

ACKNOWLEDGEMENTS

No book can be written without the help of other people: *Devon in the Great War* is no exception. I am very grateful to all the people who have been generous with their time in talking to me, or have supplied me with material for the book. This includes the staff of the various archives, libraries and museums that I mention below. I thank the following people and institutions who have allowed me to use their material: The Public Records Office, who have given me permission to reproduce Crown Copyright material and Lt-Col. (Retd) A. H. Clark, Commandant, Dartmoor Training Area for permission to reproduce the plan of Okehampton Military Camp and other information relating to training soldiers on Dartmoor. I have been fortunate in the generosity of Stuart Leslie who searched through his extensive collection of aircraft photographs and supplied me with pictures for reproduction, likewise Yvonne Hibbert, Librarian of the Radcliffe Science Library, Oxford, who has searched out key papers relating to sphagnum moss and influenza. I should like to thank Kendal Macdonald for permitting use of the picture of the placard announcing the sinking of the *Titanic*, Mrs Catherine Prance who sent me an original photograph of Flight Sergeant J. E. Prance DCM; Ian Arnold of Bideford who introduced me to Prance and the Red Baron, Mrs Sallie Hewings provided me with interesting material relating to nursing care at Exeter. I also thank the following people and organisations for their help, Arthur Clamp, Plymstock; Bryan Benge, Epsom; Syd Goodman, Plymouth; Harold Hutchings, Dartmouth; Reg Horn, Okehampton; Mark Pool, Torquay; Menon Piper, Holsworthy; Chris Robinson, Plymouth; Cyril Rushworth, Dawlish; June Whyte, Hooe; Bill Wiscombe, Lyme Regis; and George and Iris Williams of Torpoint who were very helpful in drawing my attention to the life of Beatrice Chase. Thanks are also due to the Australian War Memorial Association; Alison Mills at the Museum of Barnstaple and North Devon; the Beaford Photographic Archive, Barnstaple; the British Newspaper Library, Colindale; Dr Philip Armitage, Brixham Museum; Ray Freeman, Dartington Rural Archive, Totnes; Devonshire Regiment Museum, Exeter; Andre Gibbons, *Exmouth Herald*; the Fleet Air Arm Museum, Yeovilton; Honiton Museum; Caroline Lovell, Imperial War Museum, Lambeth; Knights of Barnstaple; Paul Davidson, Local Studies Office, Barnstaple; North Devon Records Office, Barnstaple; Paul Hambling, Museum of Dartmoor Life, Okehampton; Plymouth Local Studies Library; Public Records Office, Kew; South Molten Museum; Tiverton Library; Tiverton Museum; West Devon Records Office, Plymouth.

PREFACE

In the First World War, or the Great War as it was known before the world became embroiled in a second global conflict, tens of thousands of Devon men served in the many of the theatres of war and on the high seas, resulting in thousands of them being killed in battle. Over and above this there was an estimated four-fold number of men who were wounded. This was a terrible price for their families and the county to pay. On the Home Front in Devon important contributions were made to support the war effort, greater than many people of later generations realise as there has been a dearth of information published relating to this subject. As my text indicates, Devon was not a backwater of inactivity during those turbulent years. While Devon went to war, the war eventually came very close to Devon with the presence of U-boats attacking and sinking Allied shipping in the waters of the English and Bristol Channel.

The first chapter of my book describes some relevant events that occurred in the early part of the twentieth century, together with aspects of Devon life as it was during the Edwardian period. The five other chapters are devoted to each of the war years with selective descriptions or mention of land and naval actions involving Devonshire men. The detailed appendices I hope will be of interest, not only to the general reader, but to those people embarking in further research. In Devon the ultimate victory was received with joyous blessings and hope for a better quality of life, but this was countered in the post-war years by a downward economic spiral severely affecting agriculture and the industrial workforce. But, despite the loss of much of the best of its manhood, and the social and economic perils brought about by the aftermath of war, the spirit of Devon survived.

G. D. Wasley
East Molesey, 2000

Portent of things to come. The Cathedral School, Exeter, Cadet Corp on parade in the years before 1914. Of these cadets, and boys like them throughout Devon who fought in the coming war, many would become members of the 'lost generation', fallen victims of the Great War

1

Edwardian Devon

On 28 June 1914, Archduke Franz Ferdinand, heir to the Austro-Hungarian Empire, and his wife were assassinated by a young Bosnian nationalist while on a State visit to Sarajevo, Serbia. The consequences of this murder led to the outbreak of the Great War. Europe at this time was divided into two alliances: the Triple Alliance which included Germany, Austro-Hungary, and Italy; and the Triple Entente, a Franco–Russian alliance, with Britain entented towards the two countries. Although there was considerable diplomatic activity and political reaction resulting from the Sarajevo incident, the expected retribution came when Austria, assured of Germany's support, declared war on Serbia. There were few Englishmen who would have believed that, within a week, their country would also be at war. Russia, allied to Serbia, began to mobilise, resulting in Germany declaring war on Russia. France, allied to Russia, mobilised her army, which saw Germany declaring war on France.

The British public had no wish for their country to be involved in a war on the Continent; the British Government, although concerned about the situation, was hesitant. The attitude of both the British Government and the public dramatically changed when Germany invaded neutral Belgium. This violation drew Britain into the conflict when she submitted an ultimatum to Germany to withdraw her troops from Belgium. As there was no reply to this demand Britain declared war on Germany at 11pm on 4 August 1914. The British decision to go to the aid of Belgium was part of her treaty obligation, but also safeguarded her own interests in the British Empire.

The war had come suddenly to Britain, but the events leading up to the hostilities were not merely the result of an unfortunate assassination that had got out of control. The reader is referred here to the latter years of the nineteenth century when Imperial Germany's intentions were to become a world power – 'to take her place in the sun'. With this ambition Germany embarked on a program of building a powerful fleet of warships, while in 1905 Count von Schlieffen, Chief of the German Staff, prepared his military plan to defeat Russia and to reduce her status as a great power. To achieve this aim, the German Army would first need to subdue France. The 'von Schlieffen Plan' was to invade Belgium, wheel south and then rapidly to sweep down the flank of France, by-passing Paris, avoiding the main French defences, destroying and encircling the French army. Germany could then deploy her army to defeat Russia and not be caught out fighting a war on two fronts.

With the British Admiralty alarmed at the size and pace of Germany's naval expansion, and realising the Royal Navy's legendary superiority on the high seas was being strongly contested, the situation resulted in a naval construction race between the two powers. During June 1904, when both countries were busy with their naval building programs, the Kaiser invited King Edward VII to visit Germany and inspect the German navy. The King's host on this occasion was Admiral von Tirpitz who was obsessed with the need to increase German sea power. The admiral respected England and admired the

The historic dockyard at Devonport, where wooden ships for the Royal Navy had been built since the reign of the Tudors, was the major employer of Plymouth men at the time of the Great War. Even so, the dockyards had been run down and it was the re-arming of the German Imperial Navy in the early nineteenth century that brought about a rapid expansion to Devonport in order for it to be able to handle the building and repair of the larger warships that were now necessary if Britain was to compete on the high seas.

The picture right shows the entrance to Devonport Dockyard c.1914.

This photograph, and the two following, show the expansion of the dockyard prior to the Great War. Here the land is being excavated at the river's edge to make way for a new caisson. Steam cranes and horses and carts supplement the manual labour of the dockyard workers. The picture is dated March 1910 – note the wooden-hulled warship in the background.

On the left is the view of the South Yard looking north, showing the huge caissons in place but with much work still to be done. The photograph was taken in August 1911. In the background scaffolding encloses a warship under construction.

The photograph below, taken a few months later, shows the new shallow dock in Devonport South Yard nearing completion.

A Plymouth paddle steamer lies at anchor with the Royal William Yard in the background, c.1914.

The Theatre Royal once stood near Derry's clocktower, The photograph was taken early in the twentieth century when electric trams had been introduced. Plymouth at this time was one of the the Three Towns, along with Devonport and Stonehouse.

Royal Navy. As a young cadet von Tirpitz often visited Plymouth when the Prussian navy used the port as a supply base. The visit of King Edward was reciprocated by a hurried invitation for a German battle fleet to pay a three-day visit to Plymouth the following month.

Sunday, 10 July 1904, was a glorious day in Plymouth; the local churches and chapels quickly emptied, as thousands of people came to the Hoe and crowded the sea front to watch the arrival of the German warships in Plymouth Sound. The force was led by the battleship *Kaiser Wilhelm II*, flagship of Admiral von Koester. Following her were the battleships *Kaiser Frederick III*, *Kaiser Wilhelm der Grosse*, and *Kaiser der Grosse*. As the flagship approached its mooring it fired a 21-gun salute, with the Royal Citadel

THE WARSHIPS AT ANCHOR.

Battery above Plymouth Hoe replying 'gun for gun'; while the guns were booming four German cruisers arrived, followed by the armoured cruiser *Prince Henrich*, the flagship of Rear Admiral Schmidt. *Kaiser Frederick II* gave a salute to the British cruiser HMS *Monmouth*, later sunk at the Battle of Coronel.

The German warships anchored in Plymouth Sound while four cruisers, the *Amazone*, the *Ariadne* (the latter was sunk during the action off the Heligoland Bight early in Great War), the *Arcona* and the *Frauenlob* (both were to be lost at the Battle of Jutland), anchored on the Staddon side of the Sound. Never before had such a powerful foreign naval force visited a British port. The Mayor of Plymouth gave a banquet to Admiral von Koester and his officers. Picnics up the River Tamar were arranged for the German ratings, while in the evening the sailors were entertained at Aggie Weston's, the Royal Sailors' Rest, Devonport. The *Western Morning News* published a 'Welcome', written in German, on behalf of their readers in the Three Towns, Plymouth, Devonport and Stonehouse.[1]

Some national press editors were unhappy about the visit and, on 14 July, soon after the German fleet had sailed from Plymouth, a Member of Parliament, Scott-Montague, asked the Civil Lord of the Admiralty in the House of Commons whether his attention had been drawn to the fact that

The eastern end of Plymouth Hoe with the wall of the Citadel in the background. Wooden sailing ships can be seen at anchor in the Plym.

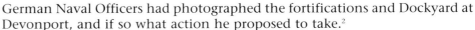

German Naval Officers had photographed the fortifications and Dockyard at Devonport, and if so what action he proposed to take.[2]

The naval visit was not the first time there had been a German presence in the history of Devon. In 1783 a detachment of German soldiers were stationed at Plymouth then moved on to Brixham. The Hanoverian troops were popular with the local people at the fishing port who preferred them to the British troops. However the Germans were later requested to leave so as to relieve the impoverished Brixham inhabitants from the burden of having to billet them.[3]

Early twentieth century Devon was a place of ancient market towns, self sufficient villages, small tenant farms, declining cider apple orchards, and up-and-coming seaside holiday resorts. Ecclesiastical Exeter was Devon's principal city. Gone, well almost, was the once thriving woollen industry and leather tanneries. Many of the metalliferous mines had been abandoned, the quarrying of Dartmoor stone considerably reduced, but there were a number of paper mills and flour mills still working. The vast Devonport naval dockyard, the economic heart of the Three Towns, was the only large industrialised complex in the county, although there were smaller works and factories elsewhere. Along the Devon coasts were fishing communities, and occasional boat-building yards. Ships with sails were a more familiar sight than boats with funnels.

Thatched-roof cottages nestled in the rural rolling hills. Throughout much of the county were austere cob-walled houses with grey slate roofs. Devon towns had their communal courtyards, dark alleys, and narrow passages bounded by old stone buildings inhabited by the poor and needy, often condemned but lived in, a hazard to public health. Homes and shops were illuminated by gas, electricity, flickering oil lamps or candlelight. Piped water was available, but not to every home, and a communal water tap was often shared between families. Water for drinking and washing was also taken from pumps, wells, and running streams. There were households with flush toilets, but many families lacked this type of sanitation and these people were reduced to digging a pit each week to bury their excreta.

The Victorians left twentieth century Devon a legacy of town halls, churches, chapels, hospitals, technical institutes, workhouses, public libraries, silent reading rooms, drinking troughs for horses, rows of terraced houses, corner grocery shops, gas works, and a network of railways. Almost every Devon town of any size had a railway station. Victorian schools were built in the green fields on the outskirts of villages, out in the remote moorland parishes and in the towns. Miles of rural countryside, of undulating hills, narrow roads, tall hedgerows, or dry stone walls, separated the communities whose lives looked inwards to their own affairs.

The tempo of Devon life was slower compared with today, the working day long, and labour intensive. Transport was usually some form of horse-drawn vehicle, as were the water tenders of the local fire brigades, although increasing numbers of motor buses and private saloon cars were seen on the streets. People cycled, others drove water-cooled motor bikes, or walked, often long distances, not for exercise, but out of necessity. Cultural interest was expressed in museums, art galleries, theatres, learned societies, choral, operatic and dramatic societies. Popular culture was predominantly found at the music hall, and in an increasing fascination with moving pictures. Communities were proud of their local brass or silver bands who led the annual carnival parade, or played in concerts at the local bandstand. Sporting activities embraced athletics, swimming, cycling clubs and motor cycle rallies. The sporting life included fox hunting, horse racing, football, cricket and tennis.

In April 1913 Smeaton's Tower on Plymouth Hoe was daubed with the slogan 'No security till you give women the vote'. Militant suffragettes painted the graffiti prior to Winston Churchill's expected arrival by yacht in Plymouth Sound.

Up to the fateful day Britain declared war on Germany, Edwardian life and Victorian values continued to influence society even though George V had been on the throne since 1910. The Edwardian period described by certain chroniclers as a time of peace and tranquility was in fact an era of growing unrest in the country, evidenced by the activities of the Trade Unions and militant Suffragettes. Since the ending of the Boer War in 1902 the British Labour movement of politics and co-operatives had grown in strength intent on improving the standard of living for the working classes. The challenge to implement social changes from the entrenched traditional ways of English life had reached Devon, but the county was not subjected to the pressures fuelled by passionate debate and agitation expressed in other areas of Britain, particularly the industrial regions.

Sweet was Devon Edwardian life for the privileged upper class, with their country estates, butlers, and champagne dinner parties, for they lived in an elegant style dictated by fashion at the Royal Court. The professional and

Lord and Lady Mildmay and their children outside the door of their home at Flete, in 1912. They represent one of Devon's wealthiest families at that time. In contrast the family in front of their small cottage on the edge of Dartmoor lived in relative poverty. Note the bicycle.

A westcountry Temperance meeting in 1913. Devon and Cornwall, with their strong Methodist roots, were considered strongholds of anti-drink campaigners.

other middle-class families also lived well, with smartly made hand-tailored clothes, live-in servants, tea parties and croquet on the lawn. The majority of Devon people however lived their lives at the opposite end of the social-economic spectrum. Even for those gainfully employed life was still a continuous struggle to maintain a 'bread line' existence, nevertheless most were loyal and well-behaved. The demon at this time was alcohol. Compared to the Victorian period the consumption of spirits and beer was falling, although still high. People in dire need were condemned to a 'workhouse' existence and the pittance of charity, but even among the impoverished there was often a genteel way of living – not all were rough or tough. A recognised and accepted life style existed between the working classes and the rest of society.[4] People lived according to their station, and it was difficult to improve one's social status. Devon in the new millennium is a more comfortable place to live compared to the early years of the last century when the general standard of living was harsh, tedious, and unhealthy. Yet, as some of the present-day Devon elders wish for the return of 'the good old days', so in the early years of the twentieth century similar sentiments were expressed by contemporaries reminiscing about their early life in Devon.

The first years of the twentieth century belonged to Marconi and his remarkable wireless waves, the developers of the motor car, and the pioneers of aviation. In 1909, only five years before the outbreak of the Great War, the French aviator, M. Bleriot, became the first person to fly across the English Channel, from Calais to Dover. This was a time when the pioneers of aviation were spending their time, and often their own money, improving the performance of their flying machines. The distinctive buzz of an aero engine was soon to be heard overhead in Devon when some of the aviators began to visit the county. It is possible that there were people in the county who saw one of these fragile flying machines even before their first glimpse of a motor car. During July 1910, George V, then the uncrowned king, arrived at Torquay to review a mighty force of three British fleets comprising 200 warships, including 27 battleships and 27 cruisers. The original plan was for the King to review the fleets at Mounts Bay, Penzance, but deterioration in the weather had delayed the Royal Yacht from sailing from Cowes. Furthermore

"Handy!" It's the "handiness" of the Ford that establishes its unbounded popularity—especially with those who have driven heavier and more cumbersome cars. And the new low price makes it as "handy" to buy as it is economical to maintain.

Runabouts £125. Five-passenger Touring Car £135. Town Car £150. Complete with full equipment, head lamps, side and tail lamps, speedometer, horn, hood, windscreen, tyre pump, repair outfit, two levers, tools and jack. All prices at Works, Manchester. More than 450,000 Fords now in service. Full particulars from—

THE TIVERTON MOTOR AND ENGINEERING CO. TIVERTON
SOLE AGENTS.
Please Note—We can supply from Stock.

the bad weather meant the fleet was forced to leave Penzance to seek a sheltered anchorage at Torbay.

The British pioneer aviator Claude Graham-White believed the aeroplane could be used as a formidable weapon of war. He had set out with a considerable amount of publicity to reinforce his views on the Government by flying his 'large wafer-like' biplane over the warships anchored in Mounts Bay. Graham-White had travelled to Cornwall by rail, bringing his dismantled Farman biplane in a special carriage. With the departure of the naval fleets to Torquay he decided to follow them but was force to land in a field at Camborne. Dismantling the Farman, and with the help of local people, the component parts were taken to Camborne railway station then sent on to Torquay.[5]   Crowds of people arrived at the resort from all over Devon to watch Graham-White take off from Torre Abbey Meadow to fly over over the warships anchored in Torbay, demonstrating how a warship could be subjected to an air attack and aircraft used as an offensive weapon.[6]

The combined fleet and (inset) the Royal Yacht anchored in Torbay, July 1910. The Royal review was originally to have been held in Mounts Bay, Penzance, but was moved to South Devon because of bad weather.

Aviator Claude Graham-White set out to show how formidable a weapon of war the aeroplane was to become.

Graham-White prepares to take off from Torre Abbey meadows, July 1910.

Graham-White was the man who made Hendon aerodrome famous (now the RAF Museum). He started a civilian flying school where Albert Ball and R.A.J. Warneford, both to be awarded the Victoria Cross, were pupils. In his book on the early aviation history of Devon, Teague refers to a Mrs H.B. Hewlett flying a Maurice-Farman biplane from Chelson Meadow, Plymouth, qualifying for her aviation certificate on 29 August 1911.[7]

During this year a number of pioneer aviators flew to Devon, following the railway line as a navigation aid, to land at Arena Park, Exeter. These men were competing in the *Daily Mail* Circuit of Britain race for a prize of £10 000. Exeter was a compulsory stop. Large crowds arrived by special trains to view these wonderful machines. One competitor was S.F. Cody the first man to fly over British soil. Cody had earlier established a reputation for his man-carrying war kites that attracted the attention of the Royal Navy. In the spring of 1904 Cody visited Devonport to demonstrate his kites but

S.F. Cody seated in his 'Cathedral' biplane at Arena Park in Exeter, 1911.

Just a few months after the Wright brothers made their historic first-ever powered flight, the Royal Navy were trialling S. F. Cody's man-lifting kite at Plymouth, assessing its role in spotting and anti-submarine duties. In the photograph on the left Cody can be seen wearing his trade mark cowboy hat while the kite is assembled on deck. The Breakwater Fort can be seen in the background. Above, the kite is aloft with the 'pilot' in a basket slung underneath. The kite is held by cable controlled through a winch on the deck of the ship.

the Admiralty were reluctant to use them. Cody flew into Exeter in his famous 'Cathedral', a complex biplane of part-bamboo construction.

Cody, born in the USA, had been a gold prospector and a trick rider in a Wild West show before he arrived in England. He dressed in a style that misled many people into believing he was 'Buffalo Bill', with whom he shared the same surname. Cody lacked knowledge of aerodynamics and constructed his machines by guesswork using materials that were condemned as being impractical and dangerous. Moreover Cody was unable to read or write and he had taught himself to fly.[8] In August 1913 he lost his life in an accident flying a seaplane.

Another aviator, Captain Clayton, travelled to North Devon by road during 1911 bringing his single-wing Bleriot aeroplane, complete with a canvas hanger, to Great Hele Barton for a demonstration flight at the agricultural show, South Molton. Soon after becoming airborne a technical fault caused the plane to crash-land into a hedge. Uninjured Clayton dismantled his aircraft and went on his way.[9] The following year the French aviator Henri Salmet, participating in a *Daily Mail* sponsored tour of Devon and Cornwall, landed at Knightshayes, Tiverton, and Barnstaple; this being the first time an aircraft had landed in North Devon.

Frenchman, Henri Salmet, stands in his aircraft after landing at Knightshayes near Tiverton during the *Daily Mail* sponsored tour of Devon and Cornwall, 1912.

Of interest to the aviation history of Devon is Peter Carden's initiative. Son of Lady Carden, living at Dartmouth, he designed a flying machine that was under constructed in the Lidstone boathouse, alongside the River Dart. Unfortunately it is not known what happened to the plane.[10]

The design and performance of aircraft was still in its infancy and very much in the hands of enthusiastic individuals like Carden when, in 1911, the British Government recognised the need to form an Air Battalion. A year later the Royal Flying Corps (RFC) was formed. The Imperial Defence of Great Britain aware of the potential threat of German military aviation, in particular their giant Zeppelin airships, began to established air bases in England. Later in July 1914 the naval wing of the RFC was transferred from the control of the War Office to the Admiralty who formed the Royal Naval Air Service (RNAS). The RNAS, whose presence was to become prominent in Devon during the latter years of the Great War possessed 40 aircraft and was given the responsibility of protecting the country against air attacks. Scouting and patrol work was then a secondary role.

Motorcycles brought cheap long-distance travel within the means of the working class, with a sidecar providing a little more comfort for passengers. Here a motorcyclist poses for a while beside a Dartmoor road, c.1914.

In rural Devon the working and social life of people was bound up with the village. Everyone worked directly or indirectly on the land, to the extent that the weather and seasons influenced their lives. Villages had their own social hierarchy and many families were interrelated. Fortunate was the villager who owned a bicycle for it gave the individual freedom to leave the restricted life of the village.

In the early years of the twentieth century many villages were on the wane, as men moved away from the land to seek a life elsewhere. An important development in 1909 was the introduction by the Liberal Government of the old age pension for everyone over the age of 70. The state pension of 75p for a married couple fell short of being an adequate basic income, but nevertheless it was welcomed. At the village of Bampton the town crier was out, bell in hand, informing the villagers where and when the pensioners could go and collect their pension.[11] Bideford celebrated the first pension day with a public meeting, speeches, and a public tea for the four hundred town elders, while at Barnstaple three hundred people qualified to draw the old age pension.[12]

There were people in Britain who believed that it was inevitable that sometime in the future the country would be at war with Germany. One respected person, Lord Roberts, had formed the National Service League (NSL), a training scheme for National Defence. To foster interest in the NSL, meetings were held throughout the country and, in 1909, one such meeting was held at Plymouth. The speaker on the platform explained to the audience the ambitions of Germany and the need for men to come forward to defend Britain, a country that was 'apathetic and peace softened'. Lord Roberts proposed that men should spend a few days training each year for the coming war. Despite the general feeling of anti-feminism and the lack of equal opportunities it did not deter some women, in 1909, to take the initiative in setting up the Voluntary Aid Detachment (VAD) as part of the Territorial Army Scheme. The objective of the VAD was twofold, to tend to the wounded and sick soldiers from the fighting front, and to care for garrison troops in the local neighbourhood. Those women who created the VAD were subjected to ridicule, an experience common to many pioneers, but this attitude changed during the war years through the magnificent service the VAD performed in carrying out their duties. This was an important factor in people changing their views regarding the value of women in society.

From its inception many people in Devon were enthusiastic about the VAD, resulting in detachments being formed throughout the county. Prior to the Great War sufficient women had qualified as VAD nurses in Devon to staff, as probationers, twenty-one hospitals within the county, excluding the medical care covering Plymouth.[13]

The foresight of Devon women in preparing for a possible war was not confined to the county towns. At the village of Cornwood, where the parish edges Dartmoor, twenty women had joined the Cornwood Red Cross Society in 1910, their uniform becoming the supreme image of care. The nurses wore white ankle-length aprons faced with a red cross, a white collar, their head covered with a soft handkerchief-style hat.[14] A few months before the outbreak of war a large mobilisation exercise was held to assess how the VAD would perform in the 'unlikely event of England being invaded.' The Devon VAD was described as one of the richest veins of the organisation and was thought to be so well prepared that, if war came, few changes of any kind would be required.[15]

To what extent Germany's military ambitions influenced the expansion of Okehampton artillery practise firing range is difficult to ascertain. There had been an army presence on Dartmoor ever since the middle of the nineteenth century. Then prior to the Boer War, Okehampton Artillery Camp was built, administered by a permanent staff. In the early years of the last century the War Office purchased 3500 acres of Wilsworthy Manor. The Camp had its own military sidings making it possible for artillery units to travel from all over the country to practise firing live ammunition on Dartmoor. Exercises were not simply a case of loading the guns and firing shells across designated areas of the moor. A recently published history *The Armed Forces on Dartmoor* describes an elaborate system of stationary and moving targets that could be made to represent advancing infantry, cavalry, guns and anything else that might appear on the battlefield. The whole apparatus was activat-

From the nineteenth century the military training area near Okehampton covered a large area of northern Dartmoor. It is still widely used for gunnery and artillery practice. In this photograph, taken c.1910, an artillery team crosses a moorland stream on its way to one of the ranges.

Troops riding out on Dartmoor from the camp at Okehampton.

ed using thirty miles of rope, with pulleys operated by teams of horses. The Okehampton Camp was also used for rifle practice when up to three thousand soldiers would participate. The summer camps bought additional trade to the local shops, boarding houses and hotels accommodating the wives of the soldiers.

The naturalised American millionaire, Waldorf Astor was elected Member of Parliament for the Sutton Division of Plymouth at the general election of 1910. At this election the Devonport Liberals adopted Erskine Childers as their second parliamentary candidate. Childers wrote the classic adventure story *The Riddle of the Sands*, concerning German preparations to invade England by crossing the North Sea. Childers remained in politics up to the outbreak of the Great War when he joined the RNAS, becoming involved in some daring actions. After the war he did not return to Devonport to resume his Liberal politics, but became associated with the troubles of the civil war in Ireland, resulting in him being executed as a rebel in 1922 by the British government.[16]

Devon people, endowed with a strong sense of loyalty to their king and country, grew up to believe in the special destiny of the British Empire. This devotion, which some may describe as patriotic passion, was influenced by school and Church. England to a Devonian meant Devon. The majority of people living in the county voted Conservative or Liberal. Left-wing politics prior to 1914 had no significant influence in Devon society.

In the early years of the twentieth century Plymouth was a port of call for ocean-going liners, a service that started in the middle of the nineteenth century. Plymouth was then an important point of emigration from where thousands of people sailed to settle in countries of the British Empire. Many would-be emigrants, arriving from Ireland, decided to go no further and settled in the Three Towns.

Shipping traffic significantly increased from the beginning of the twentieth century, for example 546 liners called in at the port during 1906. Considerable rivalry existed between the two railway companies for the conveyance of passengers and mail traffic, competition that intensified when the American Line, the premier steamship company, decided to make Plymouth one of its ports of call. Many of the passengers arriving at

Plymouth were starting on their 'Grand Tour' of Europe, by disembarking at Plymouth and travelling by express train to London. In doing so they could save a day of their vacation, rather than staying on board ship to proceed to Cherbourg, then sailing on to Southampton or London Docks. Likewise passengers whose final destination was the British Isles would also thus save considerable time.

German liners arriving in the evening tended to anchor in Cawsand Bay, their presence welcomed by the villagers of Cawsand and Kingsand who would sit on the beach to listen with pleasure to the latest Continental waltzes played by the ship's orchestra.[17] The German passenger liner, *Kaiser Wilhelm der Grosse*, made frequent calls to Plymouth. At the outbreak of war she was converted into an armed merchant cruiser and, three weeks after war was declared, the Devonport cruiser HMS *Highflyer* attacked the *Kaiser Wilhelm der Grosse*, severely damaging the ship and causing the crew to scuttle her.[18]

Among the distinguished people who disembarked at Plymouth was Lord Kitchener who arrived in 1910 after visiting America. Two days later he was received by King George V at Buckingham Palace who presented Kitchener with his Field Marshal's Baton.

For many years if a ship entered Plymouth Sound with a member of crew, or a passenger suspected of having smallpox, or any other infectious disease, they would be confined in a hospital ship. These precautionary measures were in existence during the early part of the twentieth century. HMS *Pique*, a wooden warship converted at Devonport Dockyard for use as a hospital, was moored at Jennycliff Bay in Plymouth Sound. On 8 January 1908 a number of the crew of the SS *Dunbarmoor*, that had arrived from Karachi, were taken to the *Pique* suspected of suffering from the Plague. The men were detained on the *Pique* for three weeks until they were cleared of the disease. In 1910 the *Pique* was replaced by the *Flamingo*, a converted naval sloop. The *Flamingo* had a main ward of ten beds and two separate cabins. She remained moored in Plymouth Sound until the 1930s when anyone thereafter suspected of having an infectious disease was referred to the newly-opened Lee Mill isolation hospital.[19]

Eastward along the Channel coast at Dartmouth, the small port maintained a floating isolation hospital. The *Mayfly* had been fitted out for this purpose in 1893, until she was replaced in 1923 by a paddle steamer, the *Kingswear Castle*. During her time as a hospital ship the *Mayfly* cared for thirty-three patients suffering from infectious diseases.[20]

Across the county in North Devon, Barnstaple Port Authority maintained a small French vessel the *Nyphen* as an isolation hospital ship with a four-berth ward and two convalescent wards. The only person recorded to have been detained was a seaman suffering from smallpox.[21] The *Nyphen* had air conditioning provided by wind vanes mounted on the deckhouse, feeding fresh air into the interior of the boat.

While delicate flying machines, seemingly held together by pieces of string, were to be seen more frequently in the Devon skies, the solid robust motor car was also gradually increasing its presence in the county. Prior to the Great War there were a number of Devon towns with car showrooms and garages offering service and repair work. The car was no longer a novelty prior to the war, but only the well-off could afford to own one. Motor cycles, although not cheap, were more affordable to artisans and farmer's sons. Devon roads were generally of poor quality, surfaces sometimes no more than compressed earth, and when it rained pools and puddles formed, made worse by the cartwheels that churned up the mud.

The introduction of metalled roads, hard solid surfaces, were a decided improvement. If the local borough surveyor decreed a road needed repairing, along would come a stone cracker with his hammer and sit by the roadside breaking up the stone taken from a mound by the wayside that had been delivered and dumped from a quarry. The broken stone would be impacted into the surface by a steam roller. Designated main roads at this period were narrow, bounded for many miles by high hedgerows. There

The advance of motor transport took some time to replace traditional forms of travel.
This stage coach continued to carry passengers between Kingsbridge and Dartmouth well into the twentieth century.

In 1913 a sign in a Plymouth square exhorts passers-by to see 'the wonderful display of Clyno cars at Old Town Motors'. A tram appears at the corner.

were no traffic lights or roundabouts, just a few roadway signs to aid the traveller. A straight run of road was a bonus as there were miles of twists and turns to negotiate.

Whatever the conditions of the roads in Devon they did not deter pioneer motorists from touring the county. The payment of road tolls was common and at Honiton a toll was imposed on cars entering or departing from the town. When the tolls were abolished in 1914 fires were lit in the town to celebrate the occasion. However, road tolls were collected in other places in Devon for many years.

Motor cars and their drivers were recognised as being dangerous but there was no government requirement to pass a driving test. In 1909 a speed limit of 10mph had been imposed on cars driven in Plymouth, and later, before the outbreak of the Great War, drivers were informed by motoring organisations that the maximum speed allowed through Paignton was 5mph. Early twentieth century Devon road traffic was predominantly horse-drawn, carts and wagons of varying loads, delivering everything from the Royal Mail to hauling great loads of timber. Private individuals rode on light carts or traps, or in public horse buses and charabancs. Farmers, wearing their heavy brown woollen suits and leather gaiters, usually rode on horseback. There was still in Devon, prior to the war, horse and coach services. One that ran between Dartmouth and Kingsbridge, for example, continued in service until the driver was called up to go to war,

An increasing number of holiday visitors arrived in Devon during the early years of the last century. Torquay, acknowledged as the premier resort in Britain, could boast of posh hotels and recreational facilities to satisfy the rich. Crowds of people travelled down from the northern towns of England to stay at Barnstaple or Ilfracombe, where they would be met at the railway station then conveyed to their hotels or boarding houses in horse-drawn open wagons. Holiday visitors were treated as esteemed guests, their names, where they stayed, and the dates of their arrival and departure, published in the visitors' lists of the local newspaper. The ancient port of Dartmouth, already a mecca for yachtsmen, enjoyed the status of organising an annual

Crowds on Paignton Sands, 1906. The vogue for taking seaside holidays grew as the railways reached the more rural parts of the country, with places like Torquay seen as premier resorts for the rich and famous. The photograph below reveals swimwear fashion in pre-war days.

Royal Regatta. The town published a visitors' guide informing the reader that Dartmouth was the centre from which to tour the quaint villages of the South Hams, and the plum orchards of Dittisham.

Budleigh Salterton, Sidmouth and Seaton on the south-east coast of Devon were popular places for gentlefolk to relax. Here ex-serving officers and colonials came to settle in their retirement.

The beauty and mystery of Dartmoor also began to attract visitors in large numbers. One such, more a temporary resident, was the talented artist Augustus John who arrived by caravan at Postbridge during April 1906, where his son Pyramus was born. The artist spent a happy time on the moor producing many etchings and a study of Dartmoor ponies.[22]

The second decade of the twentieth century began with the death of King Edward VII. The following year King George V was crowned and in 1911 their majesties sailed to India on the P&O liner *Medina* for the Coronation Durbar at Delhi.

In the spring of 1912 sensational news was received on the sinking of the *Titanic* while on her maiden voyage. Information of the disaster was conveyed throughout Devon by the newspapers and by word of mouth as there were no public wireless communications. The liner *Carpathia* arrived at the scene of the disaster and was able to rescue over 800 people, including passengers from the West Country. The *Titanic* was scheduled to call at Plymouth on her return voyage. In America some newspapers believed it to be a hoax, but when the radio room of the liner *Olympic*, en route for Plymouth, received news of the disaster all ship's entertainment immediately ceased.

A quartermaster of the *Titanic* on this disastrous voyage was Robert Hitchens, husband of Florence (née Mortimore), a native of the Dartmoor village of Manaton, where they were married.[23] The loss of the largest ship afloat, constructed to be virtually unsinkable, was a major blow to British esteem and the shock of the disaster penetrated through to the smallest communities. At Manaton the log book of the village school records in 1912 'Titanic Disaster has affected all, and as many lessons as possible have been founded upon it.'[24]

On 28 April the liner *Lapland* arrived in Plymouth Sound with 167 survivors of the *Titanic* crew, anchoring in Cawsand Bay. The first batch of survivors, including women stewardesses, was transferred to the GWR tender *Sir Richard Grenville*. Instead of sailing directly to Millbay Dock (Plymouth) the *Grenville* cruised around the Sound until the other two tenders with the rest of the survivors had left the *Lapland*. The delay in not immediately landing the survivors was to enable the Board of Trade to serve each person with a subpoena requiring them to give evidence before the Receiver of Wrecks at Plymouth. Millbay Dock had been closed, guarded by the police, not to bar the newspaper reporters from entering, but to prevent the *Titanic* survivors from getting out. The Seaman's Union found out what was going on and sailed out in a boat alongside the *Grenville* to explain the situation to the survivors, who responded by indicating they would refuse to give evidence unless the threat of their illegal detention was removed. The demands of the *Titanic* crew survivors were conceded and they landed at Plymouth where they gave their evidence. Arrangements were then made for a special train to be organised to take the survivors to Southampton, the home port of the *Titanic*, and home too of many of its crew.

Less than a year after the loss of the *Titanic*, news was received of Captain Scott's death near to the South Pole. Robert Falcon Scott was born at Milehouse, Plymouth. As a young naval officer he served on the doomed warships HMS *Amphion* and HMS *Majestic*.[25] Scott, leading a party of British explorers, had sailed to the Antarctic in January 1912 intent on being the first to reach the South Pole, but on arrival discovered the Norwegian explorer Roald Amundsen had reached the pole a month before. Scott, with his team lacking sufficient supplies, started their long trek across the frozen Antarctic wastes to return to base but were caught up in the most terrible blizzards. Marooned in their tent, unable to make it back to base, the gallant British explorers froze to death. Scott's failure subsequently resulted in him being criticised for not being properly prepared for the expedition and for his faulty decision making. Paradoxically Scott's failure outshone Amundsen's success. Scott and his colleagues' sufferings caught the imagi-

HMS *Majestic* in 1896. This was the vessel on which Robert Falcon Scott served as a junior officer, and which was later to become a casualty of war.

nation of the British public and this epic failure became part of the nation's history.

In Devon attitudes were changing, though ancient superstitions still prevailed. A white witch on Dartmoor was reputed to be able to stop a person from bleeding from a distance, without having to see them![26] But whatever the problems of individuals, life also had its pleasures, particularly for the young. Rag-time music, imported from America, had become popular, with the tune 'Alexander's Rag Time Band', composed in 1911 by Irving Berlin, all the rage. The young at heart danced the Turkey Trot and Bunny Hug, and the Tango arrived from South America. In Devon there were Tango teas and Tango parties, despite many disapproving of well-bred young ladies taking the floor to perform what to some people was an unacceptable sensual public exhibition. At Plymouth, Torquay and Exeter, newspaper advertisements offered tuition on how to Tango.

These newly imported dances, however popular at the time, should not be taken out of context. Most dances at this period were formal, held in hotels or public halls where it was necessary to wear evening dress or a smart suit. Entrance was by invitation or ticket, and a lady would need a partner to accompany her on such an occasion. However, the etiquette that required a women to have a dance card and to list the young beaus who wished to dance with her, had all but disappeared.

For the wealthy in Devon there were magnificent annual Hunt Balls and glittering occasions in the de-luxe settings of celebrated hotels such as The Grand in Torquay. Dancing in the Edwardian ballroom prior to the war could include dancing to the music of a lilting waltz, performing a two-step, and then taking your partner for the 'Lancers'. After a champagne supper the dancing continued, with melodies played by a string orchestra. The not-so-well-off public were not denied and, although modern ballroom dancing had yet to emerge, there were pay-at-the-door dances. In Plymouth dancing was advertised to be held every night except on a Sunday. The dances were announced by a Master of Ceremonies and the dance music played on a piano, or by a string band.

In 1913 this soldier and his wife sit peacefully in a Tavistock garden. They can have little idea that their world is about to be turned upside down. While he and his comrades are to suffer in the worst conditions encountered by any modern soldier, his wife is likely to be faced with hard manual work previously undertaken only by men.

The early years of the century saw the growing emancipation of women in British Society. The Married Women's Property Act, passed in the latter part of the nineteenth century, had given women the right to keep their own wages and whatever wealth they possessed. Later, near the end of Edward's reign, women were given the right to vote and to be elected to local government, but denied the opportunity to vote at a General Election. To pursue the issue of women's rights and to end their appalling working conditions, a Union of Suffrage Societies had been formed whose policy was to keep their campaign within the law.

One group of women however, the Suffragettes, became increasing militant and deliberately broke the law and damaged public property as a way to achieve reforms. Many of the Suffragettes, particularly the leaders, were middle-class women who gained support for their cause from various well known men, among them George Bernard Shaw.

The Suffragettes were well organised, with Mrs Emmeline Pankhurst being a leading figure. She and her daughter had visited Newton Abbot campaigning for 'Votes for Women' and became involved in the post-election riots in the town when a mob, enraged by the loss of the Conservative vote to the Liberals, attacked the militant women.

Intent on gaining support for their cause the Suffragettes became increasingly militant, although most of their activities were carried out in London. Anti-militant Suffragists had been active at Tavistock, attracting crowds to their meetings at the Town Hall without causing any trouble. However early in April 1913 the Suffragettes made their presence known for the first time in Plymouth. At Lipson telephone wires were cut, while on Plymouth Hoe they daubed a painted message on the base of the Smeaton's lighthouse and the central shelter – 'To Churchill. No security unless you give women votes'. This statement was intended for Winston Churchill, the Home Secretary, who was due to sail into Plymouth Sound on board the yacht *Enchantress*.[27] In June the following year two tubes of chloroform and phosphorous together with a message 'Votes for Women' had been posted at the main Tavistock Post Office. An immediate search was made in the other post boxes in the town revealing an envelope with a warning 'no letter box is safe until votes are given to women'.[28]

HM Submarine *A6* under completion in dry dock with another vessel of the same type. These were sister ships to the submarine *A7* which failed to surface while on trials from Devonport in 1914, and which was lost with all hands.

In Devon the fateful year of 1914 began with a submarine disaster when HM submarine *A7*, with other vessels, sailed out from Devonport on the 16 January to carry out exercises. The *A7* submerged but for some reason failed to resurface. At first there were high hopes of a successful rescue, but this did not happen and several days passed before the submarine was located four miles north-west of Rame Head, Cornwall. Entombed in the *A7* were two naval officers and nine other ranks.

At the time of the search for the submarine the naval authorities thought a seaplane would be useful in locating the vessel and Commander J. Seddon and a mechanic were ordered to fly a Maurice-Farman (No.73) from the Isle of Grain, Kent, taking a coastal route to Plymouth Sound. Commander Seddon began his flight at 9.15am, passing Beachy Head at 11.40am, before touching down at RNAS Calshot at 12.40pm. Continuing his journey, Seddon descended on the waters of Plymouth Sound at 4.40pm to be met by the destroyer HMS *Sylvia*. The journey had taken 5 hours 25 minutes.

By this time the *A7* had been located and Commander Seddon flew over the area where the doomed submarine lay, but was unable to observe it.[29] HM Submarine *A7* was one of thirteen A class boats. *A1* sank during torpedo experiments in the English Channel, *A5* was involved in an explosion on board killing five members of the crew, and *A8* foundered off the Eddystone lighthouse. The last of the class, *A13*, was the first British submarine to be fitted with a diesel engine.[30]

Life went on in Devon, with nothing to suggest, at least to the public, that war clouds would soon be forming over Europe. During the second week of May 1914, Henry Williamson, then eighteen years old, who was to become Devon's famous adopted literary son, arrived in North Devon to stay with his Aunt at a cottage in the village of Georgeham. Here the combination of the beautiful countryside, seascapes, and wildlife made a significant impression on him. At the outbreak of war Williamson, a member of the London

Devon Territorials at Ashburton on the eve of war.

Rifle Brigade, was sent to France, but soon returned to England to be commissioned. Granted leave in 1915 he returned with a friend to stay at Georgeham and thereafter made other visits to the village. After the war Williamson left the family home in London and moved to live at Georgeham.[31] Here, later, he would write his classic story *Tarka the Otter*.

Another literary visitor to Devon in the Summer of 1914 was already famous. Thomas Hardy motored from his home in Dorset to Exeter, then on to Plymouth, the birthplace of his second wife, returning home over Dartmoor. Hardy already knew Plymouth. It was here on the Hoe that, having bought a magazine from the railway station, Hardy read to his surprise the first instalment of his story *Far from the Madding Crowd*, that *Cornhill* had published earlier than planned. But that was 40 years before.

Hardy and his wife returned to Devon the the following year to visit his friend Eden Phillpotts who lived in Torquay. Hardy returned home via Teignmouth and Dawlish then stayed at the Royal Clarence Hotel Exeter, opposite the Cathedral.[32]

Except for some political comment Devon newspapers reflected little upon the impending political crisis that would lead to war. The early summer weeks were no different to previous years; shops held their annual sales, people went to work, the housewife went to her local market or had a special day out shopping at one of the larger Devon towns. Many of the younger men of Devon donned their Territorial Army uniform and went off to their summer training camps.

Jabez Wolfe had his moment of glory when, in August 1914, just before war was declared he successfully swam from the Eddystone Lighthouse to Plymouth Sound in 10 hours 46 minutes, swimming through severe thunderstorms.

Meanwhile, at Totnes, a draper was fined for having breached the Factory Act by employing two young women in his shop beyond the stipulated hours of employment, 8am–8pm, working them until 9pm.[33] At the end of July people were looking forward to the traditional August Bank Holiday, a time when many took their annual summer holiday. The newspapers and a few public speakers at local meetings in Devon referred to the warlike climate developing in Europe but in Devon there was little to signify an immediate danger. However signs of the coming conflict were to be found in the call-up of the Devon Naval Reservists, while the Government began to publish formal regulations relating to military matters.

Hoskins described Exeter, before the blitz of the Second World War, as one of the most beautiful cities in England. Before the Great War it remained a relative backwater despite its position as Devon's premier city. With a population in 1914 of around 48 000 it was never to suffer quite as badly in the Great War as the naval port of Plymouth.

CHAPTER ONE REFERENCES

1   *Western Morning News*, 11.7.1904.
2   *Western Evening Herald*, 15.7.1904.
3   *Torquay Directory*, 1918.
4   *The Deluge* (1965), Arthur Warwick.
5   *Aviation in Cornwall* (1965), Peter London.
6   *Torquay: The Place and the People* (1992), John Pike.
7   *Mount Batten; Flying Boat Base Plymouth* (1986), Dennis C. Teague.
8   *Early Aviation at Farnborough* (1971), Percy B. Walker.
9   *North Devon History* (1995), Peter Christie.
10 *Dartmouth and South Hams Gazette*, 18.2.2000.
11 *The Book of Bampton* (1998), Caroline Seward.
12 *North Devon History* (1995), Peter Christie.
13 *The Story of the British VAD work in the Great War* (1917), Thelka Bowser.
14 *The Book of Cornwood and Lutton* (1997), Cornwood Parish Project Group.
15 *The Story of the British VAD work in the Great War* (1917), Thelka Bowser.
16 *The Story of Plymouth* (1950), R. A. J. Walling.
17 *Plymouth Ocean Liners – Port of Call* (1993), Alan Kittridge.
18 *Plymouth Warships 1900-1950* (1998), Syd Goodman & Ian Ballantyne.
19 *Western Morning News*, 19.2.1966.
20 *Dartmouth and its Neighbours* (1990), Ray Freeman.
21 *Braunton* (1989), Tina Claydon.
22 *Augustus John* (1997), Michael Holroyd.
23 *The Book of Manaton* (1999), Various.
24 *Old Dartmoor Schools Remembered* (1991), Mary Stanbrook.
25 *Scott and Amunsden* (1979), Roland Huntford.
26 *Devonshire Association News* (1994), Spring.
27 *Western Morning News*, 3.4.1913.
28 *Tavistock's Yesterdays 5* (1989), G. Woodcock.
29 *History of British Aviation Vol 2*, R. Dallas Brett.
30 *HM Submarines in Camera* (1996), J. J. Tall & P. Kemp.
31 *Henry Williamson* (1995), Anne Williamson.
32 *The Life of Thomas Hardy* (1962), Florence Emily Hardy.
33 *Western Morning News*, 2.7.14.

2
1914: EARLY MILITARY MATTERS

Britain declared war on Germany at 11pm on 4 August 1914. In central London excited crowds had gathered in the streets anticipating the news that the country had decided to fight. The late-night declaration meant that the majority of people in Devon did not learn about the fateful decision until the following day, except for the minority who, possessing a telephone, received the news from 'up the line'. Official war notices were placed in the windows of newspaper offices and displayed on placards, with more detailed information published in the columns of the newspapers themselves.

Civic leaders and town criers proclaimed the news to their community, and it rapidly passed around by word of mouth. The immediate response throughout the country was a spontaneous anti-German attitude, fuelled by newspaper propaganda. Likewise, in Germany, as soon as it became obvious Britain had sided with France and Russia, there was an outburst of hatred against the British.

The war with Germany was the first time Britain had fought against a European country since the ending of the Crimean War in 1856. With hindsight it is possible to see a path which led to war, and in the years immediately before 1914 there had been clear warnings as to Germany's ambitions. But these were ignored. The British public were not well informed as to the extent of political discord among the European powers that led to the crisis of war. As was to happen two decades later, war came suddenly to a nation badly prepared. The military situation in Britain was unsatisfactory; half of the British Army were permanently out of the country and what constituted the Reserve Army, known as the Special Reserve, largely comprised young untrained troops and the Territorials, a force not liable for service abroad, but to be used for home defence. The Territorials, though of high patriotic spirit, were ill-equipped to fight against seasoned troops. But the die of war had been cast.

The weather in Devon on 4 August was fine and sunny as the Budleigh Salterton choir set off to enjoy their annual outing. Choir member Maggie Turner, dressed in her best ankle-length skirt, sat with her friends in an open charabanc to visit Haytor on Dartmoor. Returning home through Exeter the choir was surprised at the large crowd gathered in Bedford Circus and, enquiring what was happening, they were told about the declaration of war on Germany. For Maggie this was an awful shock.[1]

At West Buckland the local postman, having ridden on horseback from South Molton to deliver the mail, conveyed the news about the war to the villagers who congregated around the postman's hut.[2] At Stoodleigh, a small village near Bampton, the local cricket club was playing their annual fixture against the Knightshayes Court team. When the news of the war was received, the owner of Stoodleigh Court, where the match was being played, ordered champagne to be brought out for the cricketers, not as a cause for celebration, but because he foresaw with some prescience that many of the young men playing in the match may not be alive to enjoy it after the war had ended.[3]

A contemporary cartoon reflecting on the inconvenience of war in the holiday season. No such jokes would be published in later years, as the full horror of the war was felt at home.

THE PICNIC, SEPTEMBER, 1914.

Anxious Mother. "I HOPE WE'VE FORGOTTEN NOTHING, FRED?— SANDWICHES, SPIRIT LAMP, SUGAR, TEA, MILK, JAM, AMMUNITION, KNIVES, FORKS, REPEATING RIFLE, PICKLES, BARBED WIRE, &c., &c."

There was a sense of excitement from the very beginning with the immediate 'call to arms' on 5 August. The first Aliens Restriction Act was passed requiring that enemy nationals of military age should be interned, and others repatriated. Rumours of spies and food shortages began to spread throughout the county. Large numbers of holidaymakers who were in Devon when war was declared were caught up in a sudden exodus, but not without considerable inconvenience as the Government had, without notice, taken over the running of the railways, cancelling many scheduled services and excursions, commandeering rolling stock for the military. Those people who had planned to stay in Devon cancelled their holiday, and consequently there was a significant reduction in trade in the market towns, Barnstaple being severely affected.[4] Appeals were made to reinstate the cancelled passenger services, and although these were at first rejected, improved services were later introduced.

Another early regulation affecting civilians was the introduction of the Defence of the Realm Act (DORA), introduced and passed through the House of Commons in all stages in five minutes. DORA abolished the civil rights of people and, even though they might be unaware of this martial law, they could be charged with breaking security regulations. The police were empowered to stop and question civilians and those refusing to co-operate were liable to be detained and imprisoned.[5] The press was immediately gagged, with a double censorship imposed by the Admiralty and the War Office acting independently of each other. This resulted in only a limited amount of 'war news' being published and consequently an official Press Bureau was established that issued communiques. Any newspaper editor not conforming to the new restrictions could be prosecuted under DORA.

At the outbreak of the war the Royal Navy was to some extent already mobilised for, after the Royal Spithead Review, the fleet sailed off for exercises. Because of the political crisis reserves and regular sailors were not discharged or granted leave, as was the usual procedure. Orders were 'to be in a state of readiness', with the First Fleet being directed to sail to its war station off Scapa Flow. At the time of the declaration of war the Admiralty had signalled 'Commence hostilities against Germany' to all HM ships and naval establishments.

Whereas in August 1914 Britain's naval power, in spite of many old war-ships, was a formidable force ready if necessary to go into battle, the British Army was ill prepared. The bulk of the British Regular Army was stationed throughout the British Empire, and there were more serving soldiers in India than in the British Isles. In 1914 no British man was compelled to join the fighting services, the Government had rejected conscription, but now a large army was urgently needed to serve in France. To raise such a fighting force the British Government sanctioned the recruitment of 500 000 men.[6] This meant a major national recruiting campaign and, consequently, posters and notices appealing to young men to fight for their country appeared in newspapers, shop windows and were pasted on advertisement boards and walls.

Lord Kitchener's Appeal.

100,000 MEN REQUIRED FOR THE WAR.

NO MEN will be REFUSED who are PHYSICALLY FIT for Active Service, and between the ages of 19 and 30

OLD SOLDIERS UP TO 42

Late N.C.O.'s of Regulars and Ex-Soldiers URGENTLY NEEDED.

The first British naval engagement against the enemy occurred just two days after the declaration of war and involved the Devonport-manned cruiser HMS *Amphion*. She had orders to patrol the North Sea route from Harwich to Antwerp in order to keep the sea lanes open, but the German minelayer the *Konigin Luise* had already appeared and sown mines across the shipping routes. The *Amphion* and her flotilla sighted the enemy vessel, and within hours the *Konigin Luise* was sunk. It is probable HMS *Amphion* fired the first shots of the war. The Devonport cruiser rescued German sailors who were to become the first prisoners-of-war. On being hauled on board they looked so miserable the captain of the *Amphion* issued them with a ration of rum.

HMS *Amphion* - the first British naval casualty of the Great War. Funnel bands, just visible, were the forerunner of today's flotilla numbers, and were used to indicate the seniority of the commander in each ship.

However, within 24 hours twenty of the German prisoners were dead, as were many of the British crew, for the *Amphion* had struck a mine laid by the *Konigin Luise*, and thus HMS *Amphion* was the first British warship of the Great War to be sunk by enemy action. The news of the loss was a terrible shock, particularly to the people in the Westcountry, home to so many of her crew. An official announcement concerning the mining of HMS *Amphion* and the loss of 131 crew appeared in the newspapers, which also gave news that her captain, 16 officers and 135 other seamen had been saved.[7] The Westcountry now had its first war widows.

Throughout Devon young men came to the recruiting offices to be attested, joining those who, anticipating the conflict, enlisted before war was declared. Eager teenagers who were discovered to be too young to join up were sent home and told by the recruiting sergeant to come back on another day. Many were accepted in spite of their age. There were no lack of recruits for the Royal Navy or the Royal Marines, while recruitment for the RFC (formed in 1912) and the RNAS (July 1914) was limited mainly because of their infancy, but, as the fighting on the Western Front escalated, recruiting expanded.

A climate of enthusiasm, tinged with jingosim, was not uncommon among the would-be volunteers. For many Devon youths the war was an opportunity to escape from the tedium of life that held few prospects for their future.[8] There was also, irrespective of social class, a deep-rooted patriotism, passed on through previous generations of family and State, maintained by college, school, church and chapel. Most volunteers were conditioned to fight for King and Country, endowed with a spirit of defending the

Civilians in their working clothes, line up in front of a sergeant, waiting to be enlisted at Bideford. It is probable that they were joining the North Devon Yeomanry.

Soldiers of the 6th Devons at Woodbury Camp on Woodbury Common, 1914. These were the young men later to be described as the 'flower of Britain's youth' - thousands of them were killed. At the outbreak of war the 5th and 6th Devons were sent to Plymouth, then moved to Salisbury. Later the 6th Battalion sailed for Mesopotamia, fighting the Turks near Kut.

monarchy and the vast British Empire. These young men were quick to respond to the call of battle, unaware, as were their families, that many of them would be fighting against the most remarkable military machine of its time, the Imperial German Army.[9] Neither could they know that this was a new war, in which the technology of modern weaponry would hold sway against outmoded tactics. Devon men sent to France would be ordered into action in the deadliest theatre of war, in which for every nine men sent out five would be killed, reported missing, or wounded, a figure well above that for any other combat zone in the Great War.[10]

Not all Devon men who joined the Army served in the Devonshire Regiment, and conversely not all the men recruited into the Devonshire Regiment were Devonians. Most volunteers went into the ranks but men of a higher education, or of high social standing, were usually recruited into the officer corps. At the outbreak of war three Territorial battalions were under canvas on their annual fortnight's training course on Woodbury Common, the fine summer weather creating an atmosphere more like a fair.

News of war caused the camp to close and the men were returned to their various depots. The 7th Cyclist Battalion, based at Totnes, was quickly recalled and a detachment sent to guard various coastal areas from Land's End to Lyme Regis. Other men marched off from Woodbury to Exeter, cheered on their way by people lining the roadside. As many Devon mobilisation stations were already occupied the 5th and 6th Devons, a total of 1400 men, were sent to by train to Plymouth and crammed into the drill hall. Devoid of cooking and toilet facilities the Battalions eventually moved on to Salisbury. The Order for the 6th Devons to prepare to serve in France was cancelled and instead the Battalion, as part of the Wessex Division, embarked on HMS *Galeka* and sailed for India.[11]

The 3rd Devons, with a strength of 3000 men, were required to seek out accommodation wherever they could, ending up spread out across Crediton, Dawlish and Tiverton. During this early period even the barest necessities

Under rainy skies, on 8 August 1914, crowds at Ilfracombe cheer the 1st Heavy Battery of the Devonshire Royal Garrison Artillery marching on their way to the local railway station.

for the men were unavailable: no uniforms, no arms (except for a few old Lee-Enfield rifles only suitable for drilling), not even blankets or cutlery. The problem was only solved when four Companies moved to Granby Barracks and Raglan Barracks in Plymouth, and another Company to Mount Wise, Devonport.[12]

Plymouth at this time was swarming with regular and Territorial soldiers, to the extent that many areas of the town were out-of-bounds to the men. At least seventeen military units formed the local Order of Battle and, as mobilisation gathered momentum, so Plymouth became surrounded by training camps and the town became a central pivot of active military and naval life.[13]

In September 1914 the 10th Devonshire Service Battalion was formed. A thousand men reported, most of them wearing civilian clothes, and later 200 rifles arrived, each to be circulated in order to give every man a chance to handle one. One of the Battalion's platoons included the complete football team of the famous Woolwich Arsenal, which at least meant that the 10th Devons won every football trophy they played for.

Young men enlisted from all over Devon. At Torquay, and elsewhere, they queued up to offer to serve.[14] When the order came for the men to report for

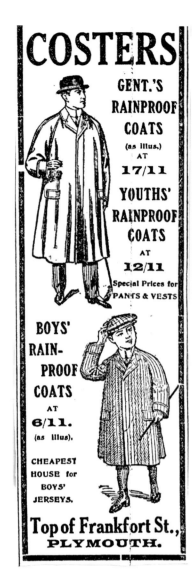
duty, the local population came out on to the streets to cheer them on. At Ilfracombe the townspeople not only lined the streets to support them but, together with the Territorials, attended an open-air service in the High Street before the men marched off to the local railway station led by a band of military and civilian musicians.[15] At Beer, a large crowd had seen off local members of the Royal Naval Reserve two days before war was declared, and the following day the crowds were out again to say goodbye to the Exmouth men of the Royal Fleet Reserve. By the end of the month three hundred Exmouth men had gone to war.[16]

At Budleigh Salterton railway station people cheered and sang as their men departed in a special train.[17] Similar scenes of cheering crowds and marching men were seen throughout the rest of the county. In North Devon, for example, in the second week of August, the rest of the Bideford Company of the 6th Devon Territorials were given a rousing send off as they marched across Bideford bridge to the town's railway station en route to their headquarters at Barnstaple. Later that day men of the Royal North Devon Hussars from the Bideford district travelled to their headquarters at Torrington.

Early images of the war were not confined to young men enlisting or going away to fight. Barbed wire entanglements and stacks of sandbags had been constructed in Plymouth and, along the coast, trenches were being dug. A large St George's Cross had been erected on every hospital amid fears of a possible enemy invasion and the possibility that Plymouth and other coastal towns may be bombarded by the enemy from the sea. This suspected threat of enemy attack increased the military presence in these areas and additional troops were stationed at Fort Bovisand, with huge guns and searchlights mounted at Jennycliff to cover the eastern entrance to Plymouth Sound, across which a boom defence had been placed. An order was issued that the lights on Plymouth Hoe were to be extinguished each night at 10pm.

Yet with all the military activity the city was full of American visitors who, on 8 August, just four days after the declaration of war, had sailed in on the liner *Oceanic*. The city gave the appearance of being under siege, with food queues forming outside many shops.[18]

Panic buying of food created shortages in the early weeks of the war. Queues outside shops, such as this one in Exeter in 1914, were not an uncommon sight.

Meanwhile the Secretary of State had signed an order for the immediate compulsory acquisition of horses and feed for the Army. This was the revival of an old English law (1692) which enacts that in time of national danger and emergency all horses and vehicles required must be surrendered to the State, with a fair market price paid for each horse taken. Heavy dray horses were to be surrendered together with their harness. Objections to the offered price could be settled in the County Court.[19] The War Book stipulated that 120 000 horses would be needed in the first two weeks of the war.

Policemen called on the horse owners and served them with a notice of surrender. The impressment required the owners to bring their animals to a stipulated location where they would be examined by an army vet. The beasts selected were classified according to their suitability for defined tasks, for example pulling a small wagon or hauling heavy gun carriages. Aveton Gifford, Hatherleigh and Kingsbridge were among the places where horses were brought for impressment. At Kingsbridge the horses were examined at the Quay at the bottom of Fore Street. On one occasion one hundred horses were selected, taken to the town's railway station, and sent to an army depot.[20]

Horses being taken to Kingsbridge quayside to be examined for possible compulsory army service (impressment). Note the garage in the background with its early AA sign.

A soldier on guard at the gates of the Citadel, Plymouth c.1914.

The commanding officer of Plymouth Fortress issued an order demanding that the town's vehicle owners must offer their transport at once to the Army Service Corps, otherwise the vehicles would be taken from them. Many owners questioned the order, unaware of the military power of compulsory purchase. The commandeered transport was used by Plymouth troops and the Western Home Defences. A common sight was to see the local civilian motor-wagons laden with stores travelling in convoy through the main streets of Plymouth.

A climate of suspicion prevailed in Devon regarding the presence of enemy agents, fuelled by the enforcement of the Governments Aliens Restriction Act. This required aliens, who were forbidden to travel more than five miles from their place of residence, to register at their local police station. Throughout Devon the police arrested all the German nationals they could locate. At Lynton and Lynmouth a number of Germans, mainly waiters employed at the hotels, including one man who had been living at Lynton for fifteen years, were taken taken to a local hall, watched by a crowd. These men were referred to as prisoners-of-war.[21]

At Torquay twenty Germans were arrested, handcuffed and sent to Exeter, while at Plymouth forty-six Germans were taken into custody. People were asked to act as informers and Lord Fortescue, Lord Lieutenant of Devon, published a notice calling on residents of the county to inform their local police station of the names of any foreigners living in their locality.[22]

Gossip created rumours of spies and subversive activities that in turn made people suspect there were enemy agents in their midst. Appeals were made for locals, particularly those who owned a gun or a dog, to go out to watch out for any suspicious characters in the vicinity of bridges or railway tunnels. Sensitive places were the tunnels at Dawlish and Teignmouth.

Special Constables were appointed in the rural areas to assist the regular police force. Among their duties at Tavistock was the guarding of vulnerable points on the London & South Western Railway, including the Tavistock viaduct. Meldon viaduct was guarded by the Royal Defence Corps. At Plymouth guards were placed on Brunel's railway bridge spanning the River Tamar, while at Exeter it was believed that an attempt would be made to

Bridges, such a Brunel's famous railway crossing of the Tamar, were considered vulnerable to enemy attack. Seen here in 1914 from the Saltash side of the river, the bridge was strategically important due to its proximity to the naval base.

Members of the Plymouth Defence Force parade at Plymouth College grounds, Mutley, in 1914. They were to serve their country in a similar way to the Home Guard in the Second World War, although their level of training and equipment was lower. These men placed themselves at the disposal of the Plymouth Fortress authorities and were used for guarding vulnerable locations in and around the city.

destroy the bridge over the River Exe. To prevent this, volunteers were recruited to maintain vigilance in the area.[23]

Anyone approaching a sentry would be challenged, and any doubts as to the credentials of an individual would lead to arrest and immediately detention and interrogation in the guard house. Marjorie Maxton lived in Devonport during 1914, in the same area as the Royal Navy's offices, near to Mount Wise Parade. She recalls armed sentries patrolling along the front of the offices, and anyone approaching the guarded area at night would be confronted by a sentry who raised his rifle and barked out the challenge 'Halt who goes there'. She also records the active pursuit of a man during the night by armed soldiers, and was told by her mother it was a suspected spy.[24] An intelligence officer stationed at Devonport spent many nights on Dartmoor investigating reports that foreigners were on the moor illegally signalling by lamp.[25]

Three weeks after the declaration of war the Germans advanced through Belgium, capturing Liége and Brussels. These dramatic events stimulated Konteradmiral Paul Behncke to submit a report to the chief of the German Imperial War Staff considering the possibility of conducting aerial warfare over Britain, using aeroplanes and airships flying from bases on the Belgian and French coasts. Behncke specifically referred to the use of airships as a means of creating maximum damage to property and morale in England. His report contained a list of towns to be considered as possible targets, including Plymouth.

Royal North Devon Hussars dismounted prior to their departure from Barnstaple station. They spent the first winter of the war on the East Coast but in 1915, without their horses, they were shipped to face the Turkish guns at Suvla Bay, Gallipoli.

A company of the 6th Devons parade before taking a route march at Barnstaple, 1914.

A real threat now existed that, at sometime in the future, the naval port could come under aerial attack from an enemy force operating from bases in north-west Europe. Reports of Zeppelins approaching South West England were collated, although most were errors of identification. As the war proceeded fear grew that eventually the German airships would arrive in this area. As it transpired Plymouth was not attacked, although there was a false alarm that brought the town to a halt.[26] Behncke had sown the seeds of destruction for the attacks that Plymouth, Exeter, and many other Devon communities were to suffer in a future war.

The British Expeditionary Force (BEF) arrived in France on 7 August 1914. The original intention was to send six infantry divisions but only four were sent at first. A fifth arrived in the third week in August, the sixth during the middle of September. Within three weeks of their arrival the British troops were involved in the first battle of the war. Faced by the advancing German army, the BEF was committed to holding a defensive line running through the northern outskirts of the Belgian town of Mons. The Germans, superior in number, attacked at 8.30am and by mid afternoon the British were forced to retreat after suffering many casualties in the region of the River Aisne.

Devon Reservists marching through Exeter in 1914. These troops, although not regulars, were sufficiently trained and equipped to be sent immediately into action.

During the fighting a brigade of Devons was moved up to a very dangerous section of the line and ordered to hold it for ten days. Here the Devons lost a hundred men as the fighting continued.[27]

The first batch of wounded soldiers from the the retreat from Mons arrived in Devon during the late Summer of 1914. They were transferred from hospital ships that docked at Southampton and taken to hospitals in Exeter, Newton Abbot, and Torquay. These were the first VAD hospitals in England to receive wounded direct from a hospital ship.

The Devon VAD organisation was extremely efficient. At Exeter for example a telegram was received that 45 casualties were being sent from Southampton, and a few hours later the men had arrived and were being treated. Later in the year, on Sunday 4 October, the West of England Eye Infirmary was notified to mobilise, and the following day the hospital was ready, equipped and staffed to receive patients.[28]

The wounded usually arrived in Devon by ambulance train, stopping at Exeter, detraining a batch of men, before travelling on to other destinations. Throughout these travels, strict security was imposed in an attempt to prevent anyone from communicating with the casualties, an exception being when the press was allowed to interview a serviceman, such reports requiring the scrutiny of the censor before being published. Station entrances were guarded and there were times when it seemed there were more soldiers than civilians waiting to get into the station.

The Retreat from Mons. Through late summer fields, past hayricks and windmills, weary British troops of the BEF makes their way back across Belgian soil.

Wounded arrive by stretcher at Friary Station, Plymouth 1914.

A Red Cross detachment at Dawlish, 1914.

Plymouth nurses and members of the Volunteer Training Corps at Church Parade, Plymouth Guildhall.

Red Cross nurses in a makeshift hospital ward in a church at Barnstaple, 1914.

At Torquay the town's newly built Assembly Hall had been converted into a military hospital, the first intake of wounded being non-commissioned soldiers. Here at the premier English resort, the young Agatha Christie worked as an unpaid hospital ward maid from October 1914 until December 1915. While at the hospital she assisted in the dispensary, leading to her studying and passing the qualifying examination in the subject. It was at this time that Agatha Christie started to write detective stories, using the knowledge of poisons she acquired working at the dispensary and incorporating the subject into her stories.[29]

Stoodleigh Knowle, the Manor House and Lycourt were private Torbay residences, owned by titled people, that were converted for use to tend wounded officers.

The magnificent Oldway Mansion at Paignton, modelled on a French palace and owned by Paris Singer of the Singer sewing machine family, was where Paris brought the dancer Isadora Duncan during their passionate love affair. Singer now loaned Oldway for use as the American Women's War Hospital, paying for it to be equipped, including an operating theatre and X-ray room. Queen Mary came to visit the servicemen at Oldway during the war, and many of those who came as wounded soldiers were so attracted to Paignton that they returned after the war for their holidays.[30]

In the course of the war 34 private houses were used as first- or second-line hospitals to care for the wounded, administered by the Devonshire Branch of the British Red Cross Society. These places were in addition to the military, naval and civilian hospitals in the county. At Clovelly Court, Hartland Bay and Castle Hill, three second-line hospitals were used for convalescent purposes or to accommodate colonial officers on leave. Some of the larger private houses became one-hundred bed hospitals, for example Peake House, Sidmouth, and Rhode Hill.

One VAD nurse who served in Devon was Sibyl Hathaway, later Dame of Sark, who with resolution confronted the Germans in the Second World War when they occupied the Channel Islands. As Mrs Hathaway's husband had enlisted with the Gloucestershire Regiment she moved from Sark in 1914 to help her sister-in-law who, acting as matron, had converted her residence into an overflow hospital at Stover Park, near Newton Abbot. Stover Park was staffed by one qualified nurse, the rest were VADs, while the family butler became the orderly.

In Plymouth five schools had been requisitioned for use as Military Hospitals, causing the displacement of hundreds of schoolchildren and resulting in many of the pupils having an extended holiday. This problem was compounded for the education authorities due to a shortage of teachers and caretakers, many of whom had enlisted. Within a month of the start of the war Salisbury Road School, now Salisbury Road Military Hospital, was receiving wounded servicemen. Crowds formed in the streets to watch the arrival of the ambulances and see the wounded transferred into the hospital. In September Red Cross trains arrived at Plymouth bringing both British and German casualties. Many of the soldiers when they arrived had wound dressings that had not been changed for days, their wounds oozing pus, often full of maggots.[31]

The panic buying of food in Devon at the outbreak of war created artificial shortages. Stocks were soon replenished and there was now plenty of food in the shops, but certain commodities had risen in price to the extent that, for many householders, this was a form of rationing insofar as they were able only to afford to buy certain items.

The shortage of male labour caused problems for the farmers, shopkeepers and other businesses and it was yet too early in the war for women to have taken over these jobs. Yet, whatever other troubles were being experienced at this time women throughout Devon were grouping together and organising committees to raise money to support a long list of causes relating to the war effort and servicemen's welfare.

The face of wartime Devon took on many guises. Barnstaple town council decided to go ahead with its annual fair, resulting in thousands of people arriving in the town, many from the surrounding communities, to attend the three-day festivities. If there was a shadow of war cast over the fair it did not deter the crowds from spending their money, as it was usual for people to save up well in advance. Among the many attractions at the amusement fair were the merry-go-round, the switchback, a scenic railway and a revolving airship. Travelling showmen were there with their kinematographs, as were conjurors, and lightning landscape artists. A special attraction was the 'Doll Lady' just 26 inches in height. In contrast 'Tango Nellie' measured 7 feet around the waist.

Here the cheapjacks and charlatans did a roaring trade, the clever 'sleight of hand' tricksters relieving innocent bystanders of their money, while quack doctors, wearing worn top hats, were skilled at duping the public into buying their miraculous medicines, claiming to cure almost every ailment. One such fraudster sold a potion guaranteeing it would turn a bottle of water into wine! But the best seller at the fair, with the exception of the delicious Barnstaple fairings, was a copy of 'The Last Will and Testament of the Kaiser'.[32]

Early in September of this year a strange notice appeared in the *North Devon Herald* for the attention of the people of Barnstaple alerting them about messages that may be dropped from aeroplanes. The messages would be enclosed in a weighted canvas bag fastened by two spring clips attached with blue, red and yellow streamers. Instructions were given that anyone finding or seeing a bag dropped from an aircraft must immediately open the bag and arranged for the enclosed message to be forwarded to the person for whom it was intended.[33]

During this month young F. T. Mullins, aged 17 years, and two other lads who worked with him on a farm at Awliscombe decided to join the Army. They set out and walked the four miles to Honiton to enlist. After being passed fit they took the King's Shilling from the recruiting sergeant who sent them by train to Exeter. Mullins was there rejected for being too young and returned to the farm but two weeks later he received a letter ordering him to report back to Exeter Barracks. Here a large marquee was erected to accommodate the new recruits. The first night Mullings slept on wooden floor with his overcoat on. Next day, after being drilled by a Boer War veteran, he was sent for further training at Crediton before moving to Warminster.[34]

The war was still less than than two months old when disaster struck another Devonport-manned warship. (It is worth pointing out here that being Devonport-manned does not mean that all serving crew members came from that place, simply that the ship's home port was Devonport. However, in the early years of the war the complement of many such ships could comprise a majority of men from one locality, perhaps from the same few streets. Only when these ships began to become casualties of war, with the resultant losses being felt in small communities, did the authorities begin to deliberately mix crews. Similar problems occurred in the Army with 'Pals' Battalions at the outset of the war). On the 22 September three elderly armoured cruisers, all recently involved in action off Heligoland, were on patrol off the Dutch coast when they were sighted by the German submarine *U9*. The four-funnelled British cruisers were steaming line ahead when HMS *Aboukir* was struck by a torpedo and started to list heavily, before going down. The Devonport ship HMS *Hogue* and HMS *Cressy* arrived on the scene and had lowered their boats to rescue survivors when HMS *Hogue* was also hit by a torpedo and sank within three minutes. The disaster was completed when the third British cruiser was torpedoed by the *U9*. The death toll of British sailors amounted to 1489, with only fifty survivors from HMS *Aboukir*'s crew of 800. The loss would have been even greater but by chance a Dutch vessel sailing in the vicinity rescued 300 men. The loss of British seamen from the sinking of these three cruisers was greater than that suffered by the whole of Nelson's fleet at the Battle of Trafalgar.[35]

This triple disaster confirmed submarines were capable of approaching their targets undetected and then could attack them with lethal consequences without risk to themselves. The success of the *U9* forever altered naval conduct of war (see Appendix A).

Among those who died were young seamen and naval cadets, no older than fifteen years of age, who had not even completed their training. One cadet who had just finished his first term at the Royal Naval College, Dartmouth, was serving on HMS *Aboukir* when his ship was torpedoed. He managed to swim and board HMS *Hogue* when she too was hit. He then swam over to HMS *Cressy* where he was hauled up from the water and, while in the sick bay drinking cocoa recovering from his ordeal, the *Cressy* was torpedoed. The young cadet managed to jump off the stricken warship and was rescued by the Dutch vessel.[36] The Commander of the U9, Otto Weddigen, returned to base where he and his crew were each awarded the Iron Cross. Three weeks later Weddigen sailed the *U9* out into the North Sea and sank the cruiser HMS *Hawker*.

In September 1914, in a dramatic demonstration of the effects of submarine warfare, the German U9 torpedoed three British cruisers the *Hogue*, *Cressy* and *Aboukir*. Here an artist depicts men escaping from the sinking *Aboukir* while her sister ships stop to pick up survivors – thus also falling prey to the enemy submarine.

A group of Belgian refugees arrive in England, 1914. The original caption provides an insight into the social mores of the time: 'Belgian refugees who are being entertained by Lord (on extreme left) and Lady Seaton at Beechwood, Plympton.'

The German Army acted punitively against the Belgian civilians, accusing them of impeding the military advance. The Germans had also been surprised by the fighting qualities shown by the Belgian Army and the plight of the Belgians had caught the sympathy of the British public, with propaganda stirring support for the 'gallant little Belgians'. The cruel measures introduced by the Germans resulted in a mass exodus of civilians from Belgium, the majority fleeing between the end of September and the middle of October. An estimated 110 000 refugees arrived in Britain, cared for by various communities organised by local relief committees, a principal body being the Prince of Wales Belgian Relief Committee.

In the South West the care of the war refugees was first undertaken by a committee set up in September, immediately appealing to the public for funds and offers of accommodation. The following month a woman representative from Exeter was sent to London, returning to the city with 120 Belgians. Thus Exeter became the first provincial centre to receive and accommodate refugees and by the end of October 800 persons had been settled in the area. The following year 3000 refugees arrived and because of the enormity of the problem the Lord Lieutenant of Devon was approached to form a Devon Committee. Later this was expanded to cover Devon and Cornwall.

In February 1916 the original Exeter Committee amalgamated with the two-counties' organisation and a new headquarters was established at 2 West Southernhay, the Exeter Dental Hospital. To assist with expenses the government made a direct grant towards the upkeep of the refugees, supported by public donations. Exeter remained the reception centre with groups of 200–300 people arriving at all hours, sometimes unannounced. The Belgians were met at the railway station and taken by city tram to one of the hostels. On one occasion a telegram was received at 10pm informing Exeter that 190 refugees had unexpectedly been sent from London and would be arriving at 2.15am. On arrival there were 235 Belgians to accommodate!

Dawlish, Okehampton, Teignmouth and Tiverton, along with many villages, were just a few of the Devon communities that offered accommodation to refugees. By the end of the war 8000 Belgians had been assisted and cared for by the people of Devon.[37]

At the time the Belgian refugees were being received in Exeter the 1st Canadian Army arrived at Plymouth. The story of the 'surprise' arrival of the Canadians began when a great convoy of ships carrying the Canadian troops and their equipment set out to sail the Atlantic. Meanwhile, on 4 October, the lst British Battlecruiser Squadron departed from Scapa Flow and, later that day, the 2nd Battlecruiser Squadron, comprising HMS *Invincible*, HMS *Inflexible* and HMS *Sapphire* with three minesweepers, also set sail. The Dreadnought battlefleet had already sailed into the North Sea and this powerful combined naval force was ordered to take up pre-arranged positions to ensure no German submarines broke out from the North Sea during the coming weeks in order to protect the convoy carrying the 1st Canadian Army.

The plan was for the battlecruiser HMS *Princess Royal* and the battleship HMS *Majestic* to rendezvous with the convoy at 8pm on 7 October. But other parts of the operation began to fall apart, starting with the withdrawal of a French cruiser, sent on escort duty to Dunkirk, thus reducing the efficiency of the Western Patrol. As the convoy sailed nearer to the British Isles, further problems were encountered. The French reported a German U-boat off Cherbourg, and a few hours later a torpedo boat of the Portsmouth Defence Flotilla sighted an enemy submarine off Culver Cliffs, Isle of Wight. The British boat fired at the submarine as it dived and just missed ramming it, but these hostile incidents necessitated a change of plan as the convoy proceeded towards Southampton. The Admiralty decided the troopships should alter course to Devonport to disembark the men and unload the military equipment there.

When the convoy reached the Scilly Isles, Admiral Wemyss began to send the troopships forward in batches. At 7am on 14 October the first ships entered Plymouth Sound, followed in due course by the rest of the convoy. This was described as a beautiful sight on a glorious autumn day. Many of the ships were decorated with maple leaves, with the troops singing and cheering.[38] The change of destination was most secret but the Plymouth townspeople, becoming aware that something special was happening in the

Devonport-built HMS *Talbot* was attached to No.12 cruiser squadron in 1914. She escorted the huge convoy carrying Canadian troops that was diverted at the last minute from Southampton to Plymouth because of a submarine threat in the Channel.

HMS *Inflexible* was one of the escorts to the convoy bringing Canadian troops into Britain. She was later engaged in the Battle of the Falkland Islands under Admiral Sturdee.

Canadian troops are brought from the convoy by tender into Plymouth, October 1914.

Sound, flocked on to Plymouth Hoe to watch the arrival of the great armada. Over 32 000 Canadian soldiers landed at Keyham.

The 7679 horses that were transported from Canada were kept on grassland at Devonport's Brickfields, and there was also a large shipment of arms, ammunition, food supplies, 127 field guns and even an aeroplane.

The change of plan had succeeded but Admiral Wemyss had not been happy with the Admiralty's decision. He thought the risk was too great, for, if an enemy cruiser (and there were unlocated German warships at sea) arrived there was nothing to prevent it from closing on the convoy at night. Once in position a German warship could have sunk many troopships before being destroyed. Had such a catastrophe occurred the effect on Canada and the rest of the British Empire in supplying troops would have been disastrous.[39]

Six days after their arrival at Devonport, a contingent of Canadian soldiers paraded on Plymouth Hoe. Later 92 trains were used to take them from Plymouth to Salisbury Plain, while convoys of their military vehicles were driven through Devon to their new camp, stopping on the way at Exeter and Honiton.

Among the Canadians who arrived at Plymouth on the 14 October 1914 were five soldiers who, during the bloody fighting on the Western Front the

Canadian troops parade at a church service on Plymouth Hoe, 18 October 1914. After the service the men sang 'God Save the King'.

48

following year, would be awarded the Victoria Cross. Major John McCrae, Second in Command of a Canadian Artillery Brigade, also arrived in Plymouth in October 1914. It was during the Spring of 1915 that McCrae, while involved in the Second Battle of Ypres, composed the immortal poem 'In Flanders Fields', published in *Punch* magazine later in that year. The poem made an immediate impact on the public and the servicemen on the front line

In Flanders Fields the poppies blow
Between the crosses, row on row...

and the poem inspired an American YWCA worker who suggested that those who wished to keep faith with the victims of war should wear a poppy to honour the dead.[40]

A convoy of Canadian army trucks waiting in Plympton High Street. They probably belonged to the contingent of the 1st Canadian Army which arrived in Plymouth in October 1914.

At Devonport the Royal Dockyard had grown into a huge industrial complex, significantly expanded to be capable of handling an increasing number of large warships. A giant cantilever crane, a landmark in the Dockyard for the next sixty years, had been erected to lift the massive guns and turrets of the Dreadnoughts. Here the 26-gun battleship HMS *Royal Oak* was built and launched in 1914 (she was sunk 25 years later by the Germans in the Second World War with the loss of 833 crew).

The employment and discharge of dockyard labour had always been a sensitive issue. Most of the 'yardees' were men, with women employed in the rope yard and flagmaking shop, and as the war progressed the workforce increased to 20 000. The main wartime function at Devonport was maintenance and repair work, with special involvement in ships associated with the Mediterranean and other distant theatres of war.

In stark contrast to this heavy industrial centre, much of the Devon landscape gave little hint of a country at war. Manaton, the Dartmoor village, comprised a few cottages with a shop, post office and public house. Here the writer John Galsworthy and his wife lived at Wingstone Farm. The effects of war came quickly to Manaton as, on the second day of hostilities, John Galsworthy was directed to take his horse to Moretonhampstead to be impressed. To his relief the steed was rejected by the army but Galsworthy was in despair that the country was at war, and agonised over not volunteering to fight, due partly to the fact he was married and to his poor state of health. Later in the war he did volunteer but was rejected as being unfit. As a way of making his contribution to the war effort he decided the money he earned from writing would be donated to various war charities, including the Motor Ambulance Fund and Belgian Relief. The writer was confronted with an unpleasant situation experienced by other British families; his brother-in-law, the Austrian artist R.H. Sauter, was classified as an enemy

John Galsworthy on his horse Peggy at Wingstone Farm, Manaton.

alien and, with his son, was sent to an internment camp. There was nothing the Galsworthys could do about it and they spent the first wartime winter at Manaton amid the moors. Ada Galsworthy, writing to the author R. H. Mottram, reflects 'the Moor is looking more beautiful than you think, I always felt sure winter was wonderful there, now I know, such bloom, blue and purple, deep rose, brown and gold, you can't help gazing and gazing'.[41]

The Galsworthys had numerous visitors, among them great figures of the literary world, guests travelling by train to Newton Abbot or Bovey Tracey where they were met by the farmer's horse and trap. Wingstone was devoid of 'modern conveniences', the rooms were lit by oil lamps or candles, and to take a bath meant using a hip bath placed in front of a blazing fire. John Galsworthy enjoyed living on Dartmoor where during the summer months he wrote many of his fine stories and novels.[42]

One long-term guest was the Belgian refugee Leon de Smet, a noted impressionist painter who spent many months at Wingstone.

In the autumn and winter months of 1914 increasing numbers of casualties appeared in the Devon newspapers, yet the censored news continued to be written in a style of guarded optimism. People were talking of the war being over by Christmas but this was no more than fanciful gossip. The school bell tolled at Manaton at 12 noon each day, when the schoolchildren prayed in silence for three minutes for the safety of relatives engaged in the war.[43]

At Exeter the military presence was largely confined to the Barracks. The city in 1914 had a population of 48 000. The ancient Cathedral's presence dominated the narrow medieval streets and byways, many of which led directly into open country. A contemporary writer describes Exeter in 1914 as living within and under the influence of a rural environment, with the city the domain of clerics, farmers, landowners, merchants and shopkeepers.

Curious Plymouthians crane forward as a stretcher is unloaded from an ambulance (a converted London bus) outside the Salisbury Road Hospital, 1914.

Yeomanry, the Royal North Devon Hussars, parade at Barnstaple before entraining for the depot at Winchester, c.1914.

The professional classes lived in large houses and employed domestic servants – a major source of employment for women and girls from working-class homes. Although the railways provided employment for many men, others worked in building and construction catering for the increasing numbers of 'out of county' people who decided to retire to Exeter. Furthermore the city had started on a slum-clearance scheme.

As Exeter began to expand, to the detriment of farmland, changes were taking place in the old social order largely inherited from Victorian times.[44]

The need for more men to enlist continued, for there were never enough soldiers to satisfy the demands of the Western Front, even at this early stage of the war. In the middle of September the famous recruiting poster of Lord Kitchener was pasted up throughout the land. It was difficult to ignore the finger of the Field Marshal pointing directly at the onlooker, with the demand 'Your Country Needs You'. In fact, the poster, which first appeared on the front cover of the magazine *London Opinion* on 15 September 1914, was designed by Alfred Leete, a Westcountryman from Western-super-Mare.

Leete had been apprenticed to an architect and had a number of illustrations concerning the Boer War published in *Punch* magazine. The famous Kitchener poster later appeared in various forms as part of a huge government campaign. The Parliamentary Recruiting Committee during the five years of war produced 54 million posters, leaflets,and other forms of advertising.[45]

Kitchener's famous recruiting poster encourages more men to join the forces. Such was the call upon new troops, and so depleting the effects of action at the Front, that conscription became necessary in order to meet the demand for 'fresh blood'.

Four months had passed since the outbreak of the war when the nation, and particularly Plymouth, were again shocked by the decisive defeat of the Royal Navy by the Germans at the Battle of Coronel. The naval engagement was a chance encounter and, although the battle might have been avoided, it resulted in the first defeat suffered by the Royal Navy in over a century.

The Coronel debacle came about when on 1 November Sir Christopher Cradock, commanding a small force of cruisers off the the coast of Chile, came across the German East Asiatic Squadron, a powerful force, commanded by Admiral Graf von Spee. Admiral Cradock decided it was his duty to commit his cruisers against the superior German warships whose gunnery was awesome. Within forty minutes the Devonport cruiser HMS *Monmouth* blew up with no survivors. Ten minutes later HMS *Good Hope* sank with all

HMS *Monmouth*, a Devonport built cruiser of 9800 tons, was sunk by gunfire from Admiral von Spee's squadron at the Battle of Coronel in November 1914. Hundreds of Plymouth families were bereaved as a result.

hands. HMS *Glasgow*, though damaged by gunfire, managed to escape, as did a British armed merchantman: no German warships were damaged, nor casualties suffered.[46] The loss of the *Monmouth* increased the list of West Country casualties, and in Plymouth numerous families were bereaved. This disaster happened during the same week that German warships bombarded towns on the East Coast of England, an act repeated in December. Where was the British Navy the Scarborough coroner asked?

A few days after Coronel two Dreadnoughts, HMS *Invincible* and HMS *Inflexible* sailed from Scapa Flow to Plymouth. Except for the Admiralty no one knew why they had been ordered to Devonport. Their arrival was to prepare them for an urgent mission to sail to the Falklands, there to intercept von Spee's cruiser squadron. It was believed the German Admiral would sail into the Atlantic to attack Allied shipping. The two British Dreadnoughts needed time at Devonport to prepare for their task ahead and the Admiral Superintendent of the Dockyard informed the Admiralty the ships would be ready at midnight 13 November. Winston Churchill the First Sea Lord responded by ordering the warships to sail on the 11 November, even if it meant Dockyard workers sailing with the ships. The Dreadnoughts sailed at the earlier date under the command of Vice Admiral Sir Doveton Sturdee.

Admiral von Spee, as anticipated by the Admiralty, had decided to attack the Falkland Islands base, but to his surprise, he encountered the combined force of Admiral Sturdee and Admiral Stoldart. The Germans attempted to escape from the British Force who pursued them and sank four warships including the *Scharnhorst* and *Gneisenau*. The Devonport built HMS *Carnarvon* involved in the Falklands engagement was awarded Battle Honours.[47] The German light cruiser *Dresden* managed to escape, temporarily eluding her British pursuers, making her way up the coast of Chile and taking refuge in the Straits of Magellan. The enemy cruiser, having been coaled and put to sea, sank the British ship the *Conway Castle*, and was eventually located by HMS *Kent*, but again made her escape, to the island of Mas

There seemed no end to the numbers of men who were willing to join up. These recruits, from the Tavistock, Totnes and Ivybridge areas have 'responded to their country's call' and joined the Devon Territorials.

a Tierra. The *Kent,* discovering the enemy cruiser once more, sent for reinforcements who shelled the *Dresden.* The Germans scuttled their warship and her crew were interned in Chile at the request of the British government to prevent them from returning to Germany to fight again. However one of the German naval officers from the scuttled *Dresden* managed to escape from the internment camp and, on his long journey back to the Fatherland, arrived in wartime Plymouth.[48]

Back in Devon the recruiting campaign continued. A novel way to persuade men to join the forces was the production of a film made by the Army Council. The film was shown at Anderton's Electric Theatre, Kingsbridge. To encourage an audience seats were free. After the interval, a colour sergeant came on to the stage to take the names of any man who came forward to offer his services.

The first wartime Christmas in Devon was celebrated in traditional style with civilians and servicemen sitting down at the table for their Christmas dinner. Whatever the inflated prices there was no shortage of food, unlike

GOD SAVE THE KING.
TO ALL MEN BETWEEN THE AGES OF 17 AND 35:
The 6th BATTN. DEVONSHIRE REGIMENT
REQUIRES ANOTHER
FOUR HUNDRED MEN
Willing to Serve Abroad.

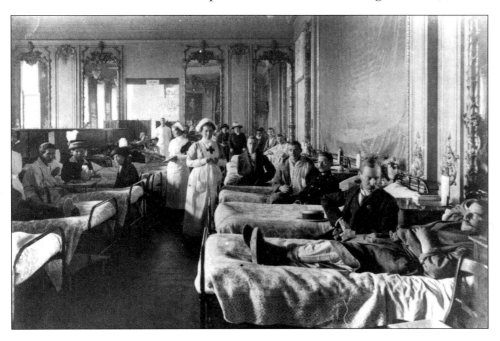

MAY Britannia's banner wave

Proudly o'er the true and brave,

Happy friendships, memories bright

Keep your heart with love alight ;

Gladness reign from shore to shore,

From this Christmas evermore.

Visiting day on the Lady Paget ward at the American Women's War Hospital, Oldway, Paignton.

Queen Mary, her entourage and medical staff at the War Hospital, Oldway. The Royal family did much to appear sympathetic, both to those fighting and those who had been wounded.

the first Christmas of the Second World War when food was officially rationed. Devon shops were full of gifts, for example at Bideford perfume sprays, cut glass toilet bottles, cigars and pipes were advertised as suggested presents. Family parlour games, piano sheet music and plenty of children's toys were being sold, but the once popular German dolls had disappeared from the toy shops.

Relatives and friends on active service were not forgotten, with parcels and Christmas cards being received at the Front. The predicted peace had not materialised and Field Marshal Kitchener was one of the few military leaders who believed the war would continue for a number of years. The Great War of attrition and slaughter had yet to be fought, but not before the most remarkable unofficial Christmas truce took place along the Western Front.

While people at Devon were at home during Christmas, the 1st and 2nd Battalions of the Devonshire Regiment spent Christmas Eve and Christmas Day in the trenches. The 1st Battalion were in waterlogged trenches outside the small shell-torn village of Wulvererghem. Christmas Eve was a bitterly cold day with snowfalls. The trenchwater froze. A private of No.4 platoon was killed by a sniper's bullet and within an hour his body was frozen stiff. At 8pm a sentry reported lights showing from the enemy trenches, then a Christmas tree with cards was hoisted from a German trench and fixed on a parapet by enemy soldiers working in full view of the Devons: not a shot was

As their part in the war effort these students from Holsworthy's private grammar school sewed up hessian sacks to make sandbags for the army. These are largely children of local farmers and tradesmen.

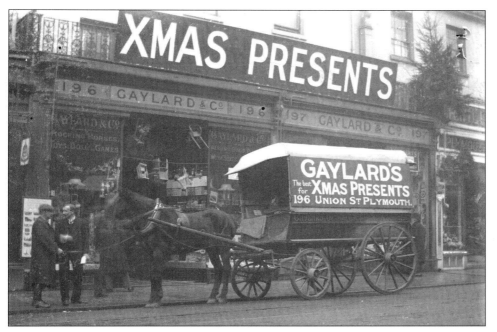

In 1914 Christmas at home was celebrated in much the usual way, although, for those with loved ones overseas, the season of goodwill must have been a muted affair. What is certain is that no one could know that the war was far from over, that four years were yet to pass with millions of lives lost, before the end.

fired. Later, music was heard, then singing by hundreds of German voices. In response the Devons started to sing hymns and carols, each side cheering the other's singing.[49]

Christmas eve for men of the 2nd Battalion of Devons was the most peaceful night of the war so far. They had no proper dug outs at this part of the front line which meant the men sleeping on the frozen trench floor. The following morning, according to routine, the Devons 'stood to', and eventually the order came for the men to stand down. The morning's task was to build up the weakest places in the parapet, the men working with fewer precautions than normally were taken.

Across no man's land the Germans worked on their trenches, standing up in full view of the Devons. Then an unarmed German soldier, a huge man wearing a green uniform, top boots and a spiked helmet slowly walked across to the Devons and called out 'you no shoot, we no shoot, Christmas for both'. Not one man moved, then, as though by command, both sides left their trenches and met in the middle of no man's land. Instead of trying to kill each other they exchanged cigars, regimental buttons and other small souvenirs. Later in the afternoon a group photograph was taken of some sixty Devons with German soldiers. As the light faded both sides returned to their trenches; the night remained silent. The following morning machine guns from both sides started up, sweeping across the opposing trenches.[50]

At the end of 1914 distant reminders of war could be seen at night in the middle of Devon when the reflection of the searchlights sweeping across the waters of the English Channel were clearly visible from the the hills at South Molton.[51]

CHAPTER TWO REFERENCES

1   *Woodbury* (1998), Ursula W.Brighthouse.
2   *Devon, Within Living Memory* (1993), DWI.
3   *Devon, Within Living Memory* (1993), DWI.
4   *Bideford and North Devon Gazette*, 8.8.1914.
5   *The Home Fronts* (1972), John Williams.
6   *The Home Fronts* (1972), John Williams.
7   *Western Morning News*, 7.8.1914.
8   *Devon Family Historian*, No 62 (1992).
9   *The Great War and the British People* (1986), J. M. Winter.
10 *The Great War and the British People* (1986), J.M.Winter.
11 *The Bloody Eleventh* Vol 2 (1994), W. J. P. Aggett.
12 *The Bloody Eleventh* Vol 3 (1995), W. J. P. Aggett.
13 *The Independent* (Plymouth), 23.8.1914.
14 *Torquay, The Place and the People* (1992), John Pike.
15 *Ilfracombe* (1996), Lois Lamplugh.
16 *Exmouth Milestones* (1948), Eric R. Delderfield.
17 *Exmouth and Budleigh Salterton* (1994), Ted Gosling.
18 Letter; dated 8.8.1914, Ref 511/1. WDRO.
19 *Bideford and North Devon Weekly*, 11.8.1914.
20 *The Kingsbridge Branch* (1997), Ken Williams.
21 *North Devon Herald*, 13.8.1914.
22 *South Molton Gazette*, 15.8.1914.
23 *Western Morning News*, 6.8.1914.
24 PC: Mrs Marjorie Laxton.
25 *In Many Parts* (1926), Lt Colonel W.R.Drury.
26 *The Story of Plymouth* (1950), R. A. J. Walling.
27 *The Bloody Eleventh* Vol 3 (1995), W. J. P .Aggett.
28 *The Story of the British VAD work in the Great War* (1917),Thelka Bowser.
29 *Agatha Christie* (1984), Janet Morgan.
30 *Historic Houses in Devon* (1987), Irene Northam.
31 *Dame of Sark* (1961), Sibyl Hathaway.
32 *North Devon Herald*, 3.9.1914.
33 *North Devon Herald*, 3.9.1914.
34 *Memoir: Private F. T. Mullins*. Honiton Museum.
35 *Submarines and the War at Sea 1914-1918* (1991), Richard Crompton Hall.
36 *The First World War* (1991), Malcolm Brown.
37 The Devon & Cornwall Refugee Committee, Ref 1262M/6139. DRO.
38 *Official History of the Canadian Forces in the Great War* (1938), A. F. Duguid.
39 *The Life and Letters of Lord Weymess* - see A. F. Duguid above.
40 *Violets from Overseas* (1996), Toni and Valma Holt.
41 *John Galsworthy* (1976), Catherine Dupre.
42 *John Galsworthy* (1976), Catherine Dupre.
43 *The Book of Manaton* (1999), Halsgrove.
44 *Victorian Exeter* (1968), Robert Newton.
45 The Kitchener Enigma (1985), Trevor Royal.
46 *First World War: The War at Sea* (1998), Paul G. Halpen.
47 *Battles and Honours of the Royal Navy* (1998), David A. Thomas.
48 *Carnaris* (1979), Heine Hohne.
49 *The Bloody Eleventh* Vol 3 (1995), W. J. P. Aggett.
50 *The Bloody Eleventh* Vol 3 (1995), W. J. P. Aggett.
51 *North Devon Herald*, 31.12.1914.

3

1916: THE REALITY OF WAR

In the early hours of New Year's Day 1915, the pre-Dreadnought battleship HMS *Formidable* was torpedoed and sunk by the *U24* off Start Point. The captain and 648 of the crew perished. The *Formidable* was the largest warship lost off the Devon coast during the Great War. Vice Admiral Bayly, the newly appointed commander of the 5th Battle Squadron, had been given the task of organising the force as a bombardment fleet. Permission had been granted for the squadron to sail from Nore, Essex, on a practice cruise in the English Channel. On the last day of 1914, the Squadron, without any destroyer protection, and accompanied only by two light cruisers, was off Portland, Dorset. During the night the warships proceeded westwards when, at 2.30am, the *U24* which had been stalking the Squadron, fired a torpedo at the last ship of the line, *Formidable*. The torpedo exploded under the dynamo room putting all the electric lights out of action.

As the battleship started to founder the weather deteriorated making it impossible to launch all but four of the warship's boats, and one of these capsized. An hour later the *Formidable* was hit by a second torpedo. The escorting cruiser HMS *Topaz* succeeded in taken off 43 men, but with the second torpedo strike it was impossible to rescue more. Two-and-a-half hours after the U-boat attacked the order was given to abandon ship, the crew scrambling over the side into freezing cold water. The old battleship went down bow first, her screws and rudder clear of the water.

One of the *Formidable*'s boats was found upside down on the beach at Abbotsbury, another landed in thick fog on 2 January at Lyme Regis, also in Dorset. Donald MacDonald, one of the survivors, records: 'For more than 24 hours they were tossed about on a stormy sea in a damaged boat which leaked so freely and shipped so freely that constant baling out by those who were able was an absolute necessity, the survivors were too weak to drop their unfortunate mates overboard so the bodies of the dead lay awash in the bottom of the boat...'. When the boat touched the beach at Lyme Regis MacDonald and one other seaman were the only men who were able to walk unaided to the nearest house. The survivors and the nine men who had died of exposure or from their wounds were taken into the Pilot Boat Hotel where the cellar was used as a mortuary. Among the dead placed on the floor was Able Seaman John Cowan whose body had been covered with sacking. As Cowan lay apparently dead, the house dog, a cross-bred collie named Lassie came and lay down alongside Cowan and began licking the seaman's face. The warmth of the dog induced Cowan's circulation, and he started to groan. The whining of the dog attracted the attention of a helper and with care and assistance Cowan revived and was thereafter able to live a normal life.

To assist in coping with the plight of the *Formidable* survivors the Mayor of Lyme Regis telephoned the Mayoress of Exeter to enlist her help in supplying items from her wartime clothing depot: shirts, socks, and vests were urgently needed for the seamen. The response was immediate, the clothes packed and dispatched to the shipwrecked sailors.[1]

1915 JANUARY 1

The GREAT RESOLUTION

FOR THE NEW YEAR

"I will be a man and Enlist To-day"

At any Post Office you can obtain the address of the Nearest Recruiting Office.

God Save the King

HMS *Formidable* was torpedoed off Start Point on New Year's Day 1915. She went down with her captain and over 600 officers and men and, although not a Devonport ship, her loss so close to home came as a major shock to the people of Devon.

Captain William Pillar. His heroic action in saving survivors from HMS *Formidable* was tinged with regret locally that his son, acting as 'tea boy' on the trawler *Provident*, was not also awarded a medal.

A launch carrying 71 men, the last boat to leave the sinking warship, drifting in the Channel, was spotted by Captain William Pillar in his trawler *Provident*. Pillar managed after four attempts in treacherous conditions to bring his trawler alongside the launch, a feat of great seamanship. All the men were saved and taken to Brixham. Captain Pillar and his crew were awarded the Silver Medal for gallantry and a sum of money from the Admiralty.[2] A group of London-Devonians invited Pillar to the capital and honoured him, paying tribute to his bravery and skilled seamanship.

The loss of HMS *Formidable* shocked Plymouth, indeed the whole country. Vice Admiral Sir Lewis Bayly was relieved of his command, although later he was appointed head of naval operations in Southern Ireland, relating to the Western Approaches. The sinking of HMS *Formidable* was disastrous enough, but compounded by serious errors of communication. Official reports of the incident did not reach the Admiralty or the Devonport Command (only a few miles from the scene of the sinking) until one-and-a-half hours after the first torpedo had struck the warship. Furthermore the position of the *Formidable* and the enemy submarine were inaccurately transmitted.[3]

Now it was shown that U-boats were able to penetrate into the south-west of the English Channel, the German Admiralty in Berlin issued a press notice stating the waters in and out of the Channel had been declared a war zone in which all enemy ships would be destroyed; vessels from neutral countries would navigate these waters at their peril. This enemy order came into force on 18 February 1915.

At the beginning of the German U-boat campaign the British Navy had few ideas of how to counter the submarine threat. Not many years before the war someone suggested a picket boat should come alongside an enemy submarine and cover its periscope with a bag, so that it could then be smashed with a hammer! Another bizarre idea was to train seagulls to alight on a periscope to indicate the presence of a U-boat.[4]

Devonport Naval Command suspected that the Channel zone in Start Bay, South Devon, was being used as a laying-up place for U-boats operating

While the press and the government suggested all was going well on the Western Front the truth was that the stalemate of trench warfare and outmoded methods of attack against new types of weapons saw casualties mounting. Here stretcher bearers give aid to a wounded soldier in a trench.

in the English Channel. In an attempt to confirm their suspicions the Royal Navy strung nets across part of Start Bay and maintained a watch. On 1 March parts of the netting were seen to sink and move with violent pulling and vibrations. The following day the Navy carried out an explosive sweep over the suspected area resulting in quantities of oil appearing on the surface of the water, leaving no doubt an enemy submarine had been destroyed.[5]

From the beginning of the war propaganda directed by the Press Bureau fostered ideas that bore little relation to the facts. Whereas the conduct of the war saw Britain and her Allies in retreat from the Germans, largely because they were unprepared, in the closing weeks of 1914 the British public were told the Allies were doing much better than the Germans. The magnitude of the German victories had not been circulated in Britain. For instance, at the end of 1914, the First Battle of Ypres had been fought in which the British Regular Army had been sacrificed, with few of the Old Contemptibles surviving. The nature of the fighting resulted in the warring armies adopting trench warfare, giving the Western Front the appearance of a great snake, extended from Nieuport, Belgium, to the Swiss frontier. Military deadlock resulted.

The theatre of the war had also broadened with many other countries joining either the Allied or the German cause. Field Marshal Kitchener needed a new army, leading to more recruitment and training for the further battles that were envisaged.

A Bairnsfather cartoon of 1915. The caption reads 'They've evidently seen me!'. Troops at the front appreciated such humour, especially from fellow serving soldiers. The appalling front line conditions were in many ways overcome through a sense of irony and black jokes.

In Exeter the good life existed for some. The Cathedral Restaurant advertised suppers, dinners and dances. Old Cognac and special Scotch whisky could be purchased – there was never a shortage of alcohol.[6]

Early in January 1915 an announcement was made that Sergeant-Bandsman Thomas Rendle of the 1st Duke of Cornwall's Light Infantry, a patient at No.2 Temporary Hospital, Exeter (the old Eye Infirmary), had been awarded the Victoria Cross. Rendle was receiving treatment for an eye injured by shell fire. News also came through that Private H.A. Saltmarsh of the Devonshire Regiment who lived at Countess Weir Cottage, Exeter, had been awarded The Distinguished Conduct Medal. Involved in trench fighting with a number of Germans, a comrade of Saltmarsh was wounded. However the Exeter man continued to fight before carrying the wounded colleague back to safety although, tragically, the wounded man was accidentally bayonetted by a British soldier and died of his wounds.[7]

Recruitment in 1915 became a relentless exercise for the military in seeking out young men and persuading them to enlist. At Holsworthy, in remote north-west Devon, a recruiting sergeant seemed to be ever-present, walking the streets of the small community.[8] Throughout Devon the recruitment campaign attracted criticism by failing to put over the true gravity of the country's position. Except for employing the King's name, many of the advertisements were more like those used to sell commercial products rather than reflecting a nation facing crisis. As one Devonshire sage put it: 'We doant think nought, Zur, o' them advertaizements and noospaper talk about going soldgering. When Guv'ment needs soldgers really sore, Guv'ment'll

THE NEW ARMY TO THE FRONT.

The bearing of the fine soldiers led by the drummer boy in this *Punch* cartoon (*above*) helped fuel the recruiting drives of 1915-16. But the picture bears little relation to the reality of trench warfare. Such jingoism meant that schoolboys were also keen to 'fight the foe' and were given every means to prepare to do so, as were these would-be soldiers from King's Nympton school (*above right*). The reality for such as these soldiers (right) at Okehampton station in 1916 was a brief training period and shipment to the Front, often with no return.

say so clear enough, like it does when it wants taxes... "Come 'long, Frank Halls, you're wanted". And when Guv'ment taps Frank Halls on showder, and sez this, I'll go right enough, but I'll not stir foot till Guv'ment zays; nor'll any man of sense this zide Exeter.'[9]

With reference to Frank Halls and his ilk, a detachment of the 3rd Battalion Devons, accompanied by a military band, set out from the Higher Barracks Exeter on an extensive recruitment campaign, visiting the communities around Torrington and the remote villages of North Devon. The marches were well planned, and villagers knew in advance of the impending arrival of the troops. The marching was on poor roads through pools of water as they passed through Yeoford, Colebrooke and Witheridge, then on to South Molton. Another recruitment march set out the following month to Holsworthy.

At Torrington the local council provided supper and organised a smoking concert for the soldiers during their two-day stay. At Beaford and Langtree the villagers hung out flags and schoolchildren came out to greet the marching men. Stubbs Cross and Shebbear were among places at which the soldiers stopped, where they made an emotional appeal for recruits.

Although some men did come forward, recruiting figures were a disappointment. A *Western Morning News* reporter who accompanied the marchers recorded the apathy of young men in the country districts; in many instances their reactions seemed, to him, unbelievable. The reporter believed some of the blame lay with farmer's sons who could have set a good example to the 'labouring classes'. At one village young farm labourers responded to an appeal to enlist by shouting out 'We'll go when the farmers sons go'. One young farmer interviewed, replied 'We will stay at home and do the farming, let others do the fighting.' Elsewhere the reply was 'Us farmers sons be going to stay at home, and look after the ground and the money.' At this interview a soldier came forward explaining he had been to the Front, and had done his share of fighting, and asked the young man 'Wont you go and help the others?' The retort was given 'I never asked him to go, I wont join, so there'. The most frequent remarks were 'I'll go when compelled', or 'When the Germans come we will join the Army.'

At one village only one man enlisted during the recruiting drive. A local retired colonel addressed the crowd explaining the country needed more men. He spoke out 'Why don't you come forward, are you always going to look with your mouths open, and let others do the work? Do not let the soldiers leave the village in contempt. What will your sons say in years to come if you do not join the Army, will none of you make any self sacrifice? Good God men of —, are you content to stop here and let others do the fighting. Do not forever hide behind the woman's skirt...'. But no one else came forward.

For the Devon's this was a waste of time and they proceeded to march to Holsworthy, then south through Ashwater, St Giles on the Heath, to Lifton, then on to North Tawton. Later the troops boarded a train and returned to Exeter. In six days they had brought in a total of 54 recruits.[10]

However, the reluctance of some men to enlist did not reflect the true patriotic commitment of Devon. Henry, Thomas, Frank, James, William and Fred were the six sons of John Lazarus who lived at Bampton.[11] All the sons were serving in the Army, while John Burnett, of High Street Barnstaple, whose brother was killed in France, had five sons serving, as were the five sons of Mrs Blackberry of Sidwell, Exeter.

As the recruiting drive of the 3rd Devons was finishing, so the ill-fated Allied Dardanelles campaign began on 19 February 1915. The British sent their older battleships for this operation so not to weaken the force of the Grand

HMS *Ocean* sails out of Plymouth Sound, the Breakwater in the background. On 18 March 1915, in the Dardanelles Straits, she struck a drifting mine and sank. Most of her crew were saved.

Fleet in the North Sea. The main Allied plan was to go forward, bombard and capture the Gallipoli peninsula, before advancing to Instanbul (Constantinople). This first meant an Allied Fleet proceeding through the neck of the Dardanelles, a narrow stretch of water that flows between the peninsula and the Asiatic shore.

Entering the 'Narrows' was to enter the jaws of death as eleven Turkish batteries created a formidable defence, together with numerous minefields. Here in these dangerous waters many ships were lost, including, on 18 March, HMS *Irresistible*, probably having struck a floating mine. Fifteen minutes later the Devonport-manned battleship HMS *Ocean* sank after being mined, although most of her crew were saved. The failure of the naval attacks on the Turkish fortifications guarding the Narrows did not deter the Allies. After a pause they landed an expedition, mainly Australian and New Zealand troops, on the southern end of the peninsula, and at Suvla Bay, assisted by an Allied naval force. However the landings were achieved at a high cost and, by the end of May, three British battleships had been lost, all torpedoed, including the Devonport-manned HMS *Goliath* and HMS *Majestic*.

The 3rd Marine Brigade, landing on Y Beach on 25 April, included a Plymouth Battalion of Royal Marines and, following the landing at Suvla, the Royal 1st Devon Yeomanry and The Royal North Devon Yeomanry arrived as reinforcements.

The Australian and New Zealand Army Corps (ANZACs) who were involved in the Gallipoli campaign were under the Command of Lt-General Sir William Birdwood, one of the few commanders who emerged with credit from the Gallipoli disaster. He had Devon connections. Sir William was born near Poona, India, and as a young boy he came to live at his grandfather's house in Bideford, later returning to India. In 1918 he would travel to Devonport to say goodbye to the Australian troops who were going home.

At the end of the war he was given the Freedom of the Borough of Totnes, the sixth member of the Birdwood family to receive this honour. The Birdwoods were an old South Devon family, from the South Hams, and on one occasion Sir William stayed with Lord Mildmay at Flete house before travelling to Exeter to present a captured German gun to the city on behalf

of the Australian government. This was presented as a token of gratitude for the kindness and hospitality shown by the people of Exeter to the Australian troops that passed through Exeter by train. Later Sir William was promoted to Field Marshall and created a peer, taking the title Lord Birdwood of Anzac and Totnes.[12]

The Gallipoli campaign turned into a military disaster with thousands of troops gaining a precarious foothold on the shore of the peninsula. After suffering appalling losses through poorly planned attacks and disease, Allied troops were evacuated in one of the few well-organised operations of the campaign.

The Royal Marines and various detachments of Devon Yeomanry fought at Gallipoli. This scene of British troops 'going over the top' against well-prepared and resolute Turkish defences was typical of the poor tactical awareness of Allied leaders.

Off the Devon coasts the German submarines were becoming increasingly active. On 7 March the collier *Bengrove* was sunk five miles off Ilfracombe by a U-boat. Five days later *U29* one of the latest and largest enemy submarines sank the French steamer *Augustus Consell* off the South Devon coast, and in early April a U-boat captured the *Lockwood* and sank her 25 miles south of Start Point.

Although people in Devon learnt little of the real war from the censored press, a glimpse of reality of the dreadful conditions, particularly on the Western Front, was conveyed by servicemen home on leave, and through the increasing numbers of maimed and wounded men in hospitals. But the stark horrors faced by the fighting men prevented many of them from telling their relations and friends the gruesome facts. What had appeared to the general public were newspapers and pictorial magazines that, having passed the censor, conveyed the war in terms of heroic photographs and lavish illustrations of 'successful' battles.

A postcard typical of those to be sent from home to serving soldiers at the Front. Most civilians had little idea of what fighting men were facing, whilst the soldiers themselves often kept the worst from their friends and family back home in order not to worry them.

In Devon the roll of honour of those who had lost their lives was being recorded while various committees continued to collect money for endless good causes. The war to many people was far away across the water and the reality of war was suppressed both by the government and by the media. Often news of the death in battle of a well known member of the community would appear in the local newspaper next to a report of a wedding, detailing the venue for the honeymoon. The lives of the majority of civilians in wartime Devon went on without a significant change. In 1915 Okehampton had a population of 3000 people and, except for those few who found it necessary to move away to find a satisfactory job, the

A middle class Devon drawing room from c.1915. The gas fire and the bric-a-brac, the candlesticks on the mantlepiece and picture rails are typical features of this period. Here guests would be taken – not to the 'living room' which was for everyday use.

majority of inhabitants lived their daily lives oblivious of much going on in the world beyond the boundary of their town. And this was true of many rural communities in 1915.

Social life in such places often centred around the place of worship, the family and the home. In gas-lit drawing rooms, family and friends would gather for an evening's entertainment. Out would come board games such as snakes and ladders, while card games were very popular, but never played on a Sunday. Many households possessed a piano, perhaps handed down through the family from Victorian times, and often with a good collection of sheet music. Folk would stand or sit by a piano listening to a young talent play their practice piece, then others took their turn to play a solo or a duet. Every one was expected in some way to participate, perhaps by singing a song, reciting a poem or comical verse. Away from the home, church and chapel social events were always very popular, as were chapel suppers.

Public entertainment at Okehampton was limited, almost non-existent. At Christmas time a visiting showman arrived and set up his props to stage a pantomime at the Pretoria in North Street. Okehampton did have a small cinema that charged a halfpenny entrance fee, one penny for a better seat. The women who took the tickets at the door was also the usherette, and played the piano to accompany the silent films. During the interval she appeared again to sell drinks and sweets to the patrons. There were times when the owner interrupted a show to announce a film had just arrived from London and would immediately be screened as part of the programme, at no extra cost.

While the regular drinkers in the local pubs had, by tradition, their personal drinking mugs hung up in the bar, so the daily customers of the Okehampton barber-shops had their own shaving mugs. The barber employed a lather-boy whose job was to work up a good lather with a shaving brush then to call over the barber to close shave the customer with an open razor.

Wartime Okehampton streets maintained a quietness only disturbed by the passing of horse and cart. If a person was known to be ill, straw was sometimes laid on the road outside their house to deaden the noise of the

Fore Street, Okehampton.

traffic.[13] Soldiers occasionally ventured into the town from the nearby artillery practice range.

Until 1915 children living in the country districts attending Okehampton Upper School were expected to provide their own dinner, but now with the introduction of the Schools Meals Service they were for the first time able to have a hot dinner on the premises. A meal for a pupil cost one-and-a-half pence, and might comprise bacon, potatoes, a pudding, and a cup of hot cocoa.

The consequences of war came to Okehampton in a way not uncommon to other Devon communities. When, for example, a large hay rick caught fire at Southcott Farm, near Higher Bowden, a message was sent to Okehampton Fire Brigade. Due to the shortage of horses, many having been impressed by the army, there were none to pull the fire engine. Eventually two horses were found, belonging to the farmer whose rick was burning, and the problem now was to muster sufficient firemen as most of the regular force had gone to war.

Okehampton shopping arcade is a famous feature of this market town. Note the maid in her pinafore and lace cap.

One of Okehampton's Home Front war efforts was their weekly collections of eggs donated by the townspeople. These eggs were sent to the military and naval hospitals as a treat for the wounded men. Egg collecting was not however unique to Okehampton as many Devon communities participated in this voluntary scheme. People would sometimes pencil their name

Mr and Mrs Sydney Simmons receiving members of the local Bible Class at Castle Lodge, Okehampton, in 1915.

and address on the egg shell and in return receive a note of thanks from the recipient. The total number of eggs collected each week was published in the local paper and, although there was never any serious competition between communities, each strived to show the other they had managed to increase the number of eggs collected. In the first week of August 1915, 540 eggs were collected from the people of Okehampton.[14]

The conduct of the war did not deter all summer visitors from coming to Okehampton for a holiday. For the war-weary the town was an ideal place to relax, with delightful local walks and trips on to Dartmoor. Furthermore the town had a good train service. One particular visitor during 1915 was William Crossing, who had published a celebrated guide to the moor. He gave a lantern slide lecture 'Dartmoor Story and Tradition' using 100 glass slides to illustrate his talk.

The genteel life continued, at least for some, with a Miss James taking her Bible Class to visit the gardens at Okehampton Castle, and to have tea. The town's workhouse children enjoyed a visit to Exmouth.

In the daily routine of life petty crime continued with people being brought before the local magistrate. One Okehampton man was charged with being drunk in charge of a steam roller![15]

On the Western Front the 2nd Devons were involved in the Spring Offensive, fighting in the area of Neuve Chapelle. General Haig ordered the attack regardless of loss, resulting in heavy British casualties, with the Devons being shelled by their own artillery. This was at the time when there was a shortage of heavy guns and shells, creating a public outcry in Britain. The so-called shell scandal resulted in the establishment of a Ministry of Munitions, with David Lloyd George appointed as Minister, who demanded a more vigorous and efficient prosecution of the war.

News came through that John Smyth, a native of Teignmouth, had been awarded the Victoria Cross on 25 April 1915, at the Battle of Festubert. He was the only British Officer in the Indian Army to win the VC on the Western Front.

Not far from Teignmouth, on the south-east coast of Devon, the roll of honour at Exmouth includes the name of R. Warneford, one of the most celebrated recipients of Britain's highest award for valour. Warneford's feat in destroying the first Zeppelin airship over enemy territory stirred the nation. Lieutenant Warneford of the Royal Naval Air Service had been ordered to take off and intercept three Zeppelins returning from a mission over England. Flying a French Morane monoplane, Warneford sited Zeppelin LZ37 flying over Ostend early on the morning of 7 June 1915. The enemy airship opened fire on the Morane which gained height and then closed in behind the Zeppelin. Switching off his engine Warneford glided his plane above LZ37, close enough to release his small bomb load on to the airship, causing the LZ37 to catch fire and crash. From the blazing inferno the Zeppelin's coxswain had an incredible escape, falling through the roof of a convent on to an empty bed.

Sub-Lieutenant Rex Warneford VC.

The explosion from the stricken airship caused the Morane to go out of control but Warneford manage to right his aircraft and fly homewards. Following the submission of his report Warneford was recommended for an award of the Victoria Cross.

Although not a native of Devon (Warneford was born in Darjeeling), as a young man he had applied to join the submarine service through the Royal Naval College, Dartmouth. He failed to make the grade, subsequently joined the Army, then transferred to the RNAS. The Devon connection came about through his mother who settled in Exmouth.

Shortly after his heroic exploits over Ostend, Warneford, along with an American newspaper reporter, were on a test flight in a Farman F27 when the aircraft went into a spin, and both men were killed. Warneford was buried at Brompton Cemetery and, on the day of the funeral, his coffin was drawn to the graveside by Royal Naval Blue Jackets Almost 50 000 members of the public looked on as a party of fifty servicemen fired a salute in his honour. His mother received his Victoria Cross with the rare blue ribbon, given to those in the naval service.[16]

Prior to the Great War Francis Brett Young a local doctor wrote *The Deep Sea* describing the hardships and tragedies he encountered in his work as a medical man among the Brixham fishermen and their families. Before the war

Brixham harbour as it looked around the years of the Great War. Shortage of labour and restrictions placed on traditional fishing grounds by the Admiralty posed problems for what was an essential industry throughout the Westcountry.

the Brixham trawler industry was flourishing, with 150 apprentices, many of whom went on to gain their skipper's certificate at the age of 21. Dickenson records there were 213 Brixham trawlers registered in 1910.[17] Most of the fleet spent the year fishing in the Bristol Channel but when war was declared the trawlers were ordered back to port. Two hundred Brixham fishermen were recruited to serve in HM minesweepers and other vessels guarding the Orkneys and Scapa Flow, while Scotsmen were sent down to Brixham. The wartime shortage of men meant at least twenty fishing boats were idle, and lack of crews forced some owners to sell their boats. Fish landed at Brixham quay was sold at a high price. The Devon Sea Fisheries Committee proposed to the Board of Agriculture and Fisheries that Belgian refugee fishermen could be employed on the trawlers, with one Belgian assigned to each boat. This proposal was at first rejected, the Ministry arguing this would appear to favour one group of foreign nationals over others. The Ministry also thought there would be a problem of distinguishing genuine Belgian subjects from German spies. Later however there was a change of mind and the Belgian refugees were allowed to crew Brixham trawlers.[18] The presence of Belgian fishermen and their families in Brixham in the Second World War is due largely to the connections made during this time.

Later in the war the British Government urged fishing boat owners to take considerable risks in order to supply the country with fish, and this they did with terrible consequences. In Brixham, for instance, only 86 trawlers remained at the end of the war, many having been sunk by U-boats.

Whatever the threat from an enemy submarine or mine, ocean-going liners continued to arrive in Plymouth, although the number of calls had been reduced compared to peace time. A continuous flow of rail and road traffic transporting weapons and supplies arrived at Devonport to be loaded on to ships. Among the deliveries were Short 184 seaplanes destined for the Dardanelles theatre of war.[19] Plymouth was a prohibited area for aliens, but this did not prevent the occasional foreign subject from entering the town. At a lodging house on Plymouth Barbican the owner was prosecuted for failing to register the name and nationality of a person deemed to be an alien.

Vigilance was maintained by the Plymouth Watch Committee regarding Sunday trading in the town, any lapse in the law governing the sale of goods on the Sabbath and the shopkeeper was reported to the police, and most likely prosecuted. In King's Street, Plymouth, there were thirteen second-hand clothes and shoe shops which the Watch Committee insisted should be closed on a Sunday.

On 7 May 1915 worldwide reaction and outcry occurred when a U-boat attacked the passenger liner *Lusitania*, torpedoed and sunk within 18 minutes off the coast of southern Ireland with the loss of 785 passengers, including 124 Americans – the total loss of life numbering 1198 souls. There was considerable controversy about the enemy attack, the Germans claiming the *Lusitania* was carrying ammunition. This was denied by the British, although later it was confirmed that she was. The loss of American life alienated public opinion in the United States and was a contributing factor towards the country later declaring war on Germany.

Plymouth was a naval port, awash with soldiers. The 3rd Battalion of the Devons moved its headquarters to Plymouth during May 1915, with four companies accommodated at Granby Barracks, one at Mount Wise, and four others at Raglan Barracks. Any soldier not having previously visited Raglan Barracks may have wondered where he had arrived, for the barracks were built with verandas due to a mix up with the plans. Consequently a design meant for the Indian Army was used to construct barracks in Plymouth.

The increasing number of wounded service men admitted to the Plymouth Military Hospitals caused a shortage of fruit, eggs, flowers and confectionery that were supplied to the patients to make their stay in hospital more pleasurable. To rectify this situation Mrs Waldorf (Nancy) Astor proposed the setting up of a central supply depot in Plymouth to create fairer distribution of gifts being donated for the welfare of the wounded. Nancy Astor lived at Elliot Terrace, a Grand Victorian House on Plymouth Hoe that after the Second World War she gave to Plymouth City Council. During the Great War Lady Astor would take wounded servicemen out in her motor car to drive over Dartmoor to Princetown, returning via Tavistock to treat them to tea at the Bedford Hotel. This charitable aid to convalescing was also carried out by car and bus drivers in other places in Devon.

Along with many British troops, Plymouth was temporary home for colonial soldiers such as these from the Indian Army. Far from home, and in a climate alien to many of them, these troops fought bravely on the Western Front.

Wounded men of the King's Own Yorkshire Light Infantry at the military hospital Salisbury Road, Plymouth, 1915.

Collecting money for the numerous war charities was shared by communities throughout Devon. In Okehampton, 7 August was 'Forget Me Not Day' when a collection was made for the Mayoress of Exeter's Hospitality Fund to provide food for soldiers travelling on troop trains on their way to the Front. Such a good cause was not without rancour. The intention was that Okehampton should make the first collection, each donor being given a small flag, but two days before the collection took place South Molton held their 'Forget Me Not Day'. This annoyed people in Okehampton who resented having to take second place. To counter this they set out to collect a record sum of money, but were subdued when Exeter sent them so many flags that seemed impossible to sell them all. However the local Okehampton organisers prepared their flag day well, recruiting twenty women and Red Cross nurses who starting early in the morning on house-

In 1915 pupils of Holsworthy Grammar School baked and sold cakes in order to raise money for the war fund.

to-house calls. By 10am they had sold over 1500 flags and more were now
required. To satisfy the demand 600 more flags intended for Hatherleigh
were commandeered. Further flags were sent by train from Exeter and, within an hour of them being received, another 900 flags had been sold.[20]

Throughout Britain the number of volunteers recruited began to falter, at a
time when replacements were urgently needed to fight on the Western
Front. An indication of the Government's intentions to resolve this problem
was the introduction of the National Registration Act to enlist all men
between the ages of 18–41. Lord Derby was given responsibility to organise
a scheme to encourage men to enlist who would then be placed on a reserve
list to be called up later. The 'Derby Scheme' did to a degree increase the
number of volunteers, including married men whom the Government

RURAL LIFE UNDER WAR CONDITIONS.

As more young men joined the
forces, rural communities suffered.
This cartoon of 1915 humorously
portrays the result.

pledged would not be called up before the single men. There was however a warning given by Lord Derby that unless sufficient men volunteered and enlisted compulsory recruitment would be introduced.

The 3rd Devons recruiting detachment were out again touring Mid and South Devon. At Preston one man had come forward to enlist at the rally despite being blind in one eye! The Devons then arrived at Torquay with the hope of enlisting 100 men from a large crowd assembled in Torre Square. The throng was addressed by Sergeant Rendle VC who came to support the recruiting drive. Rendle was very forthright asking the public to boycott shops that employed men of eligible age. The day's effort produced only nine men. At Babbacombe and St Marychurch there were no volunteers, but however disappointed the recruiting party may have felt, Torquay already had 2000 men serving, six per cent of the population.[21]

Tiny Horrabridge station where the King and Queen alighted in 1915.

On 8 September King George V and Queen Mary arrived at Devonport station in the royal train for a two day visit. This was the first public engagement of the royal family in the country since the outbreak of war. The visit started with an inspection of troops and the presentation of decorations at the Brickfields, Devonport, followed by an extensive tour of seven military and naval hospitals visiting sick and wounded servicemen. At the end of the first day the King and Queen departed in the royal train from Devonport to Horrabridge, near Tavistock, for an overnight stay, returning the following day to Plymouth North Road station. During the morning more hospitals were visited, with the afternoon devoted to naval affairs at Devonport. After a parade and a march-past in double fours, the King presented nine men with the Distinguished Service Medal, before proceeding through the Dockyard, passing HMS *Prince of Wales* and the *Royal Oak* to visit various workshops.

The visit completed, the King and Queen returned to North Road Station and travelled back to Horrabridge.[22] The following day the royal couple were taken to Exeter, the first time in a hundred years a reigning sovereign had entered the city, the last being King George II. The royal visit was supposedly a close guarded secret, but the people of Exeter found out and crowded the streets to greet the King and Queen who had continued their visiting of wounded servicemen in hospital.[23]

September 1915 was in many ways an eventful month in wartime Devon. On one particular day the Dutch steamer *Fresia*, having sailed from Buenos

No.3 Military Hospital, Exeter at around the time of their visit of Exeter hospitals by King George and Queen Mary in 1915. Above: patients and staff at the hospital.

Aires and bound for Amsterdam, called at Plymouth. Among the passengers was Reed Rosos, a very sociable Chilean widower who made friends with the British passengers. He was in fact a German naval officer in disguise who, having served on the scuttled *Dresden* at the Battle of the Falklands, had escaped from a Chilean internment camp. At Plymouth the passengers and crew of the *Fresia* were interrogated by naval intelligence officers and Rosos was screened and cleared by security. The Dutch ship sailed to Amsterdam, where Rosos, after some difficulty, secured an entry visa into Germany and arrived home in October. After submitting his account of the fate of the *Dresden* to the German naval authorities he went on to serve in a U-boat in the Mediterranean. The man who thus successfully avoided British naval intelligence was in fact Wilhelm Carnaris who eventually became an Admiral, and was later appointed by Hitler as Chief of the Abwehr – the military intelligence service of the High Command of the German Armed Forces. Although 'Hitler's Spy Master', Carnaris was involved in a plot to assassinate the Nazi leader and was arrested and later hanged in April 1944 just before the end of Second World War.[24]

During the period that Carnaris was outsmarting British Intelligence, Plymouth was the focus of attention concerning the remarkable case of Princess von Wrede, suspected of being a German spy who was in residence at the Grand Hotel, Plymouth Hoe. The investigating officer was Lieutenant Colonel W. F. Drury, a Royal Marines Officer attached to the intelligence department of GOC, Devonport whose responsibilities included the investigation of suspect aliens.

It was by chance that a woman staying in Plymouth whose husband worked at the passport office asked Drury 'what have you done with the Austrian Princess?' Drury's immediate reaction was that it was a flippant question, until she told him her husband had recently refused issuing a passport at Folkestone to a certain 'Princess' von Wrede on grounds of her undesirability. The lady in question had now been in Plymouth for some weeks, yet the local police had failed to notify the intelligence department at Devonport of her presence. That an undesirable alien of enemy birth and social prominence had been allowed to enter a prohibited area in wartime, and then permitted to live there for a considerable time in full view of the activities carried out in Britain's second naval port, was incredible.

Drury decided to investigate the situation. He examined the Grand Hotel register that confirmed the Princess was indeed staying there, but had registered as 'de Wrede', rather than as 'von Wrede'. Drury checked with the police station who was unaware of the Austrian's presence as she had not registered with them. The next day Drury, the Chief Constable of Plymouth, along with two senior Scotland Yard officers attached to Devonport Intelligence, went to the Grand Hotel and arrested von Wrede on a charge of having contravened DORA.

While the lady was being interviewed at the police station Drury and the two police officers examined her hotel room, finding among her possessions thousands of pounds worth of jewellery and a number of letters. The 'Princess' appears to have been careful in not carrying any incriminating correspondence, but she had made one mistake in not destroying a torn sheet of paper. She was duly charged, although allowed to return to the Grand Hotel.

Drury decided to contact the French secret police in London who were very co-operative. Confidential information revealed the French government had given the 'Princess' French naturalization papers in error. Drury now realised the lady was not a French subject, but a potentially dangerous enemy alien.

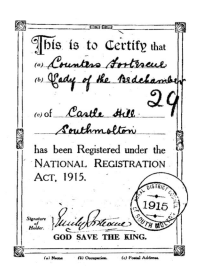

In 1915, under the Registration Act all citizens were required to carry formal identification.

Lt-Col. Drury, 1915.

On the day of the hearing the Plymouth court was packed, as the case had created considerable interest. The accused, a very attractive woman, captivated the Bench and the Chief Constable from the moment she entered the court. The subsequent proceedings were most irregular, as the French Consul was allowed to address the Bench from the solicitor's table, submitting that the accused was a friendly alien. He then picked up his hat and umbrella, pleaded a pressing engagement, and left the court. The Consul had not taken an oath, entered the witness box, or been questioned.

The Magistrate then indicated a verdict had already been decided and did not wish to hear any more evidence, but Colonel Drury insisted he should be allowed to give his and he related to the court the dramatic story of the accused woman. It turned out that she was born in Austria of humble parents and married a Polish citizen. Then Prince von Wrede appeared in her life and, in due course, her earlier marriage was annulled and she married the Prince. Her first husband, not accepting the annulment, took his case to the Court of Appeal in Paris who upheld the original marriage. Legally the Princess von Wrede remained the wife of a Polish national and, as he had never been a naturalised French subject, it was impossible for his wife to be one. This was the error admitted by the French police, yet the accused had been represented by the French Consul!

Drury then referred to the scrap of paper that the accused had forgotten to destroy. It was written in German from an officer in the Prussian Army, thanking her for the hospitality at her Villa La Ferte, in Northern France, during the German advance. The German officer wrote 'it was pleasant to come across a German house in France'. As this was read out in court it seemed that everyone held their breath, but the accused and her solicitors sprang to their feet in protest. The Chairman of the Court announced Drury's evidence was irrelevant and refused to allow a French detective to give evidence, but Drury insisted on continuing.

The public present were now with Drury, who produced evidence that the daughter of the accused was the wife of von Bissing's Chief-of-Staff (von Bissing being the German Governor of Belgium), while her mother lived unfettered in Plymouth, having lunch on board a warship and, with the permission of the Foreign Office, in direct communication with the wife of a senior enemy army officer.

It seems incredible, but the Plymouth Bench imposed a fine of £5 and permitted the accused to return to the Grand Hotel. On hearing the decision she exclaimed 'Five pounds, there is twenty for your poor box.'

The GOC and Chief Constable of Plymouth had power to evict her from the city but could not be persuaded to do so, and she remained at the Grand Hotel for several weeks more at a time when HMS *Warspite* had left Devonport in secrecy. The accused then left for London.

Drury later contacted Scotland Yard but the 'Princess' had vanished. Five years later Drury received information from the French secret police that she had been re-arrested in France.

Drury describes this strange wartime episode in a memoir, stating that he believed there was a powerful hidden hand that for some reason protected the 'Princess' against British Intelligence during the Great War.[25] On leaving the Royal Marines, Drury eventually became the Mayor of Saltash, Cornwall.

Life in the village of Upton Pyne, three miles from Exeter, had hardly been affected by the war. The Lott family who lived there ate well. Wild rabbits were plentiful and there was often rabbit stew or pie for dinner, and like many villagers, the Lott's kept chickens. There was never a shortage of meat, the butcher calling each week to take the weekend order and delivering it on Saturday night.

Children in rural areas were often better fed than their urban counterparts, although hunger was ever-present. They suffered too with absentee fathers – a high percentage of whom were in the services or engaged in increasingly demanding work on the land. This school group from Meavy parish are dressed typically for school-children of their day, the girls in pinafores and the boys with lace collars and hobnail boots. Disease and sickness due to poor diet was ever-present and infant mortality high.

The village policeman was also a gamekeeper and supplied Mrs Lott with pheasant and partridge eggs to be hatched and reared under her hens, the young birds then returned to the gamekeeper.

Men would travel from Exeter to collect finches eggs to be sold to bird fanciers, and the gamekeeper, aware of this, would keep a watchful eye on the finches nests, and substitute sparrow eggs for them.[26]

Village schoolboys wore woollen jerseys, often knee breeches, and hob-nail boots (the latter repaired by the village blacksmith). School girls wore pinafore dresses, black woollen stockings and laced boots. The girls grew their hair long with plaits or curls and when they grew older, worked their long hair into a bun.

At the beginning of the war the fashion was for women's skirts to be long, nearly touching the ground. Convention ruled they would never dare show their ankles, and when they had to walk over wet or muddy ground they developed a knack of lifting their long skirts sideways, with a sudden flick, to prevent them from getting wet. Clothes were wool in winter, cotton and silk in the warm weather. Throughout the war years women continued to

A little Miss in her Sunday best, 1915.

From her broad-brimmed hat and veil to her high button boots, this lady is every inch a fashion statement of her times – 1915.

adopt the latest fashion, assuming they could afford to. The quality and cut of material reflected the wearer's social status. Women's clothes were usually handmade if money was no object, a dressmaker calling at home to take the client's measurements, and to agree fittings before the garment was finished.

Although the age of massed-produced fashion clothes was yet to come, ready made clothes were sold in towns and larger villages throughout Devon. The working classes tended to make most of their own clothes; rolls of material to be found in abundance in shops and local markets. Many homes in Devon had a sewing machine, dress skills and needlework being learnt from mother and taught at school. Clothes were usually passed down to the younger children, and often worn until they were in tatters.

A significant change in fashion during the Great War was the style in womens footware. The accepted convention was for women to wear the Victorian laced boot, but these were being discarded for fashion shoes that began to appear in the shops. Such changes in fashion during the war were a reflection of the social climate in Britain acknowledging to a degree the new found place of women in society. Emancipation saw those very long skirts gradually worn at a shorter length and, in the immediate post-war years, worn above the knee.

Munitions shortages continued to cause considerable concern, due partly to the rivalry between the War Office and the Admiralty, combined with insufficient TNT to supply all the requirements for the shell programme. Munition factories were producing stacks of empty shell cases but the discord between the two services as to what mixtures should be used for filling the cases resulted in the production of live shells being seriously affected. Colonel Less whom Lloyd George appointed to assist him as Minister of Munitions, returned from France and reported to the Minister on how British Artillery failed to make any impression on the enemy barbed wire defences.

An essential component in the process of manufacturing cordite for shell cartridges was acetone, produced by the destructive distillation of wood. Up to the outbreak of war there was only one small factory in the country

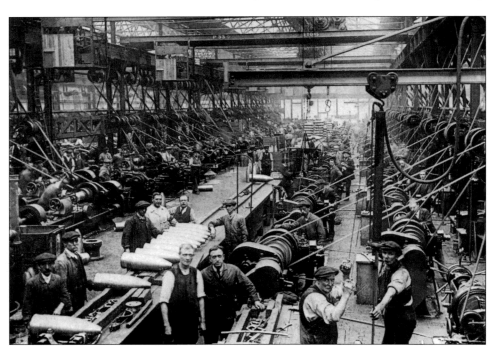

A British munitions factory in the early years of the war. Later, particularly in activities such as polishing shell casings and filling shells, women were employed. The poor working conditions and the effects of breathing in toxic chemicals made many such workers chronically ill.

involved in acetone production, in the Forest of Dean. To increase production the Ministry built two more factories, one of them was Messrs Kynocks, an HM explosive factory at East-the Water, Bideford. However because of the shortage of timber and the very large quantities of wood required to produce acetone, Britain had also to import it from America. The matter was urgent, for without acetone there would be no cordite for shells.[27]

Bristol was chosen in the South West as a munitions centre, but this was partly decentralised, with local committees set up in the area including Exeter and Torquay.[29] At Exeter groups of local people formed small companies with the purpose of obtaining government contracts for the production of munitions. One such was the Willey Vulcan Works on Haven Banks.

Most of the munition factories were located in London, the Midlands and the North of England, but as production increased others were set up in Devon, at least one in Plymouth, another in Barnstaple, while Heathcoat's of Tiverton sent the first consignment of 18-pounder shell cases to Bristol on 13 November 1915.[30]

Women munitions workers at Willey's Vulcan works on Haven Banks, Exeter

Officers of the 3rd Battalion of Devons mingled with the crowds at the annual Tavistock Goose Fair, while a car with recruiting posters pasted on it drove around the town and the Band of the Royal Medical Corps played popular music. As the officers sauntered through the fair they came across a group of young men in civilian clothes resulting in another fourteen young men being recruited for the Army. In Plymouth the Mayor made a public appeal, at the request of Lord Derby for volunteer workers to seek out and canvas every male resident in the town eligible for service with the colours.[31]

The part played in the Great War by the Royal Marines is rarely given the prominence it deserves when compared with the Army and Navy. Royal Marine detachments from Plymouth were in action in various theatres of war and a Plymouth Battalion formed part of a Royal Marines Brigade that served in Belgium and France. The Marines had by this time fought at the Battle of the Falklands, and would be at Jutland. Colour Sergeant Hill of the Royal Marines Light Infantry lived in Devonport and served on HMS *Devonshire* of the 3rd Cruiser Squadron patrolling the North Sea. Hill kept a diary while on board ship and records, on 17 September 1915, that the Admiral visited the ship leading to rumours that the *Devonshire* was Plymouth bound. The warship was under two hours' notice to sail from Rosyth with a destroyer escort for Devonport to take on board a cargo of gold bullion for delivery to Halifax, Nova Scotia. As the *Devonshire* approached the Straits of Dover progress was extremely slow as minesweepers had not finished sweeping the area and it was considered unsafe. The cruiser had to be guided through narrow channels marked with buoys. Fog delayed her entering Plymouth Sound, luckily for Sergeant Hill who won the kitty for stating the correct time the *Devonshire* would pass the Breakwater Lighthouse. The cruiser proceeded up the Hamoaze to the coal jetty, then moved to the Prince of Wale's basin. The bullion arrived by train escorted by 28 Marines with the gold packed in wooden boxes, each with two seals. HMS *Devonshire* left Devonport with her precious cargo, escorted by three destroyers. Although fearful of a possible enemy attack, the sea journey was uneventful and they reached their destination safely.[32]

Much of the local commerce in Devon centred around markets. These were set up not only in the towns and villages but at cross roads leading to remote village communities, and here farmers would bring their cattle and chickens

Looking down St Paul's Street, Tiverton, c.1915 Much of the housing in this area was built by the Heathcoat family in order to house those working in their textile factory.

and small goods to be sold. Tiverton held a great cattle market on the second and last Tuesday of each month, with two fairs for cattle, horses, and sheep on the first Thursday. Tuesday's covered market had areas for selling pigs and other livestock, together with butchers' stalls. Here farmer's wives would congregate to sell their dairy produce.

Tiverton, with a population of 10 000 inhabitants, was served by a wide range of trades and craftsmen catering for a traditional lifestyle that in the future years would all but disappear. For example in 1915, the town had 15 boot and shoemakers, 8 watchmakers, 16 tailors and 22 butchers. The spiritual needs of the community were attended to by over twenty places of worship.

The dominant presence in the town was Heathcoat's textile factory which provided employment to a great number of people. Heathcoat's were good employers with consideration for their employees' welfare. Here in rural Devon, Tiverton had a technical science and art school for day and evening classes where ironwork skills were taught, and education extended to decorative work and foreign languages, with scholarships offered to Tiverton's famous Blundell's School.

Communications were well established with a five-mile branch line connecting Tiverton to the Great Western Railway main line, while the Exe Valley line from Exeter to Dulverton passed through the town. Tiverton carriers operated from the Prince Regent and Queen's Head hotels twice a week and travelled on to Exeter. Buses met every train arriving at Tiverton station.[33]

As with other Devon communities many of the town's young men were away in the services. The 4th Battalion of the Devonshire Regiment had their drill hall at Tiverton, complete with instruction quarters, a miniature rifle range and billiard room.

Near Tiverton is the village of Bampton, famous for its annual horse fair. It was here that Anketell Moutray Read was born and enjoyed part of his education before entering Sandhurst Military College. He also attended the United Services College at Westward Ho! Captain Read fought at the Battle of Loos and, by his outstanding bravery and leadership during an enemy attack in which he was mortally wounded, he was awarded the Victoria Cross. During the Great War at least 300 men of Bampton served in HM forces.

In south Devon anti-German feeling was being expressed at Buckfastleigh with criticism that four of the Abbey managers were Germans who were not naturalised.

Christmas 1915 outwardly was a sombre affair compared with the previous year, with shopkeepers not making the usual colourful and interesting window displays. The war cast a shadow over Plymouth, few people were out carol singing, and the very wet weather did not help. Yet there was more money being spent this holiday time than ever before. The butchers and poulterers who had laid in large stocks were sold out, even though prices were up.

If anyone needed to be reminded that the country was at war, they need only look at the vast numbers of servicemen on leave in the streets. The Post Office was extremely busy with an increase in letters and parcels to be sent, many to serving men overseas. To cope with the Christmas mail at a time when 200 postal workers were serving in the forces, the Plymouth sorting office employed 300 women. At Exeter uniformed postwomen made their first appearance on the city streets.

Sailors at the Naval Barracks, Devonport were granted leave, but most of them remained at the base. The Royal Dockyard was almost closed down for the 'Yardies' to enjoy a break. In contrast very few soldiers stationed in barracks around Plymouth were granted leave.

On Christmas day a large hospital ship arrived in the Sound and began to discharge the sick and wounded from Serbia and Macedonia to be taken to the military hospitals.

Considerable attention was paid to Christmas celebrations for the wounded and the Christmas day menu at the Royal Naval Hospital, Devonport, included turkey, venison, veal, beef, and ham. Concert parties visited the hospitals but in the rest of the city, except for a few cinemas that remained open, there was no other public entertainment until 27 December when the pantomime and music hall shows commenced.[34]

The Western Front in 1915 saw a great Allied offensive known as the Second Battle of Ypres in which the Germans first used poison gas. The month-long battle achieved few territorial gains from the enemy, but resulted in the death and wounding of over 60 000 Allied soldiers and 35 000 Germans. It was often more by accident than by good military planning that ordinary soldiers survived.

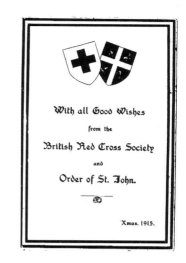

With all Good Wishes

from the

British Red Cross Society

and

Order of St. John.

Xmas. 1915.

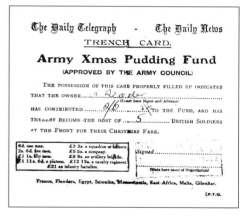

The Daily Telegraph - The Daily News

TRENCH CARD.

Army Xmas Pudding Fund

(APPROVED BY THE ARMY COUNCIL)

THE POSSESSION OF THIS CARD PROPERLY FILLED UP INDICATES THAT THE OWNER............................

(Insert here Name and Address)

HAS CONTRIBUTED.......9/6........TO THE FUND, AND HAS THEREBY BECOME THE HOST OF.......5.......BRITISH SOLDIERS AT THE FRONT FOR THEIR CHRISTMAS FARE.

6d. one man.	£3 3s. a squadron or battery.
2s. 6d. five men.	£5 5s. a company.
£1 1s. fifty men.	£9 9s. an artillery brigade.
£1 11s. 6d. a platoon.	£12 12s. a cavalry regiment.
	£21 an infantry battalion.

Signed.............................

(State here name of Organisation)

France, Flanders, Egypt, Salonika, Mesopotamia, East Africa, Malta, Gibraltar.

[P.T.O.

Nurses and patients celebrating Christmas in a decorated ward at Salisbury Road Hospital, Plymouth.

CHAPTER THREE REFERENCES

1 *Express & Echo*, Exeter, 2.1.1915.
2 Captain W. Pillar, *The Devonian Year Book*, 1916.
3 ADM 131/78: Station Records Plymouth, PRO.
4 *Look at Submarines* (1969), Edward Young.
5 *History of the Great War, Naval Operations* Vol 2, H. Newbolt.
6 *Express & Echo*, Exeter, 2.1.1915.
7 *Bideford & North Devon Gazette*, 23.2.1915.
8 PC: Menor Piper.
9 *Ordeal by Battle* (1915), Frederick Scott Oliver.
10 *Bideford & North Devon Gazette*, 23.2.1915.
11 *Western Times*, Exeter, 11.5.1915.
12 *Khaki and Gown* (1941), Field Marshall Birdwood.
13 *Through the Mists of Memory* (1995), R. C. Richards.
14 *Okehampton News*, 6.8.1915.
15 *Western Times*, Exeter, 24.6.1915.
16 *Exmouth Journal*, 10.6.1999.
17 *A Living from the Sea* (1992), M. G. Dickenson.
18 *Brixham Western Guardian*, 7.1.1915.
19 *Royal Naval Aircraft: serial and units*, (1992), Sturtivant and Page.
20 *Okehampton News*, 13.8.1915.
21 *Western Evening Herald*, 1.9.1915.
22 ADM 131/ 92: Station Records Plymouth, PRO.
23 Untitled Newspaper cutting, 10.9.1915, Okehampton Museum.
24 *Carnaris* (1979), Heine Hohne.
25 *In Many Parts* (1926) Lieut-Colonel W. P. Drury.
26 *Growing up between 1900–1920*, (1996), Grace Horseman.
27 *War Memoirs* (1933–1920), D. Lloyd George.
28 *History of the Ministry of Munitions* (1921–1922), Vol 2.
29 *History of the Ministry of Munitions* (1921–1922), Vol 8.
30 *Heathcoat's Day Book*, Tiverton Museum.
31 *Western Evening Herald*, 29.10.1915.
32 *Colour Sergeant, RM*, C. G. Hill. Ref. 80/35/1. IWM.
33 Tiverton (1914), *Kellys Directory*.
34 *Western Morning News*, 27.12.1915.

4
1916: Jutland and the Somme

The first Sunday of January 1916 was observed in Britain as a special day of intercession and united national prayer for those involved in the war. Every religious denomination combined to participate in the solemn event and muffled church bells rang throughout Devon as a tribute to the men who had been killed in the war.

Throughout the county the police were forever vigilant to ensure the wartime regulations were being observed by the civilians. Those failing to comply faced prosecution. A Plymouth woman was fined by a local magistrate for driving a car with headlights in Tavistock Road, Plymouth, within six miles of the coast, thus contravening an order under DORA.[1] A person would also be liable to prosecution under the same order if found sketching within this stipulated distance of the sea.

Although the popularity of the silent moving pictures was increasing, both theatre and music hall continued to flourish in Devon during the war. Theatre audiences put up with uncomfortable conditions that would not be tolerated today. At the Theatre Royal in Exeter, for instance, the floor was stone and wooden forms served as seating, although for a small extra charge a patron could purchase a seat with a back rest. Watching a play standing up was quite usual. The Theatre Royal had a tradition of attracting the leading actors of the day, the supreme Sir Henry Irving played at the Royal to packed houses. During the Great War famous West End theatrical stars would perform at 'Flying Matinees' at the Theatre Royal, arriving in time for the curtain to go up at 2pm and, when the play finished, travelling back to London to play in the evening performances, returning to Exeter the following day![2]

The Palace Theatre, Plymouth, a comfortable variety house with a capacity of nearly 2000, played to full houses, many of the artistes touring the circuit that took in Exeter and Torquay. Here the great stars of English music hall appeared on the stage, the likes of Marie Lloyd topping the bill on a salary of £130 a week. Here, at this handsome theatre of red plush seats and gilded woodwork, the comedian 'Little Titch' appeared, his trademark elongated boots looking like the floats of a sea plane.

The popular eccentric comedienne Nellie Wallace sang comical songs to her audiences, one of them beginning 'I don't like my mother's pie crust, eat it no, I'd rather die thus...' – such was the humour of the day!

The shortage of male acts during the war years at the Palace resulted in some shows being produced as revues. During the first week of April 1916, Lily Langtry, whose star was falling, performed on the middle of the bill at the Palace as a speciality act, being paid £14 for the week.[3] This was not Miss Langtry's first visit to Plymouth as she appeared in 1898 as Lady Teazle in *The School for Scandal* at the St James' Hall in Union Street.

Before King Edward VII died, Lily Langtry, one time mistress of the monarch, had turned her attention to Prince Louis of Battenburg, the British Sea Lord, who also became infatuated with her. It was Prince Louis who had warned the Admiralty of the potential danger the Cressy class cruisers were

MARY PICKFORD
"The World's Sweetheart"
FAMOUS PLAYERS LEADING ARTISTE
CONTROLLED BY J.D. WALKER'S WORLD'S FILMS LTD

Mary Pickford, star of the silent screen.

A band concert on board HMS *Hibernia* during the Great War.

exposed to but there were strong rumours circulating that, because of his German ancestry, he was an agent of the German secret service.[4] The antagonism shown towards him resulted in his resignation as First Sea Lord. He changed his name to Mountbatten and took the royal title the Marquess of Milford Haven.

The Grand Theatre Plymouth, standing opposite the Palace Theatre and the Alhambra, Devonport, staged many productions during the war with a patriotic theme. Jokes were told about the Kaiser and the artistes on stage would call out to the audience, urging any of the young men present to join the services. The imposing Theatre Royal, Plymouth, continued to present plays, but the travelling production companies were declining. One of the consequences was the creation during the war of the Plymouth Repertory Group, staging its productions at the Old Mechanics Institute. This was one of the earliest repertory theatre groups formed in Britain.[5]

Performances in theatres and music halls were alive and thriving, but the light entertainment of the once popular Victorian concert parties, of minstrels and pierrots performing in Devon parks and on seaside piers, were losing their appeal to the public, as were lantern-slide shows. However, it would be some years before they entirely faded out as a public entertainment.

Moving picture shows were a growing form of entertainment in Devon during the Great War, and it was from this period that the national anthem was played regularly in cinemas and theatres at the end of the show.[6] Film shows, once presented as a novelty, caught the public interest and a number of film companies were set up to make moving silent films. Travelling showmen toured the county presenting film shows in rented halls, or at fairgrounds. Many towns had at least one permanent picture house, for example at Bideford, Exmouth and Holsworthy. At Budleigh Salterton films were shown at the Masonic Hall, West Mill.

In the small riverside town of Dartmouth, then with a population of only 4000, there were two cinemas during the war where the film programmes featured newsreels with glimpses of the fighting on the Western Front.

A travelling showman at Torbay, 'King of the Electric Moving Pictures'.

Many picture houses were converted buildings or rooms, adapted for the purpose of projecting films. The Electric Cinema at Devonport, a converted hall, was one such popular picture house where during the interval a singer with a three-piece orchestra entertained the patrons.

Purpose built cinemas sprang up in the middle-class areas and in Mutley Plain the Cinedrome had opened in 1914, decorated in white, cream and red, fitted with a 18-feet wide screen. The Cinedrome possessed it own generating station, so unreliable was Plymouth's electricity supply.[7] In Union Street, near Stonehouse, another purpose built cinema was designed to accommodate 1500 people.

Most of the silent screen films shown were American, the leading actors becoming film stars, adored by the public. Although many films were 'single reelers', when D. W. Griffith produced his epic films with a cast of thousands, many reels were needed to carry the story.

Until 1916 the War Office and the Admiralty were responsible for recruiting and processing the volunteers. Lord Derby's policy of increasing the numbers of men enlisting had not been successful, resulting in the introduction of the first Military Services Act (1916). Compulsory enlistment was now introduced for single men and childless widowers between the age of 18–41. Later, by a further Act of Parliament, the age limit was raised to 51 years. Exemption from service was given to clergymen, essential war workers, the physically unfit, and approved Conscientious Objectors.

The Military Service Act was on the statute book within nine days of it being introduced in the House of Commons. To ensure that men did not escape service each borough town in Britain held regular tribunals, set up under the Act, comprising members of the local authority and representatives of the military. These tribunals sat throughout the remainder of the war. Many applications for exemption came from employers seeking immunity for their staff on the grounds they were indispensable. Other men argued their case of domestic responsibility. The military complained the tribunals were too lenient; other tribunals were accused of being too severe, particularly to the Conscientious Objectors. The meeting of the tribunals and the fate of the applicants were reported in local newspapers

The first meeting of the Okehampton tribunal was held on 25 February 1916. As the officer representing the military authorities was unable to attend a local Alderman deputised for him. From the six Okehampton men applying for exemption two were refused, the other four were referred for reconsideration at a later date. The owner of a Temperance hotel at Okehampton, also a builder and coal merchant, applied for his son to be exempted as he was indispensable in helping to run the premises and coal trade. His application was rejected.

A local hairdresser also applied for exemption for her son who managed the hairdressing business since her assistant had enlisted. The application was put back for 6 months.[8]

Later in the spring Heathcoat's of Tiverton submitted the names of fourteen male lace-makers to the local tribunal, the company arguing that fifty of their employees had already joined the army, and lace-making was a skilled job. The tribunal rejected all the applications of the single men, whereas the decisions regarding the married men were postponed, or conditionally exempted. The Tiverton factory had been under scrutiny, prior to the tribunal, and four HM Inspectors of factories from the Home Office arrived at Heathcoat's to enquire what the company was doing with regard to employing girls and women to replace the male lace-makers. It was explained to them that twenty-three women were performing work previously done by men. Soon after there was a follow-up visit by two superintendent Inspectors of Factories to enquire if more female workers were being introduced into the lace-making rooms.[9]

The acute shortage of labour was a real concern for farmers in the Dartmouth area. They complained, among other things, they were unable to properly trim their hedges. Furthermore costs had increased with farm labourers now being paid one pound a week, whereas up to the outbreak of war wages were 70p a week. There had been a move to employ women on the farms, but the local farmers were unhappy about the prospect, arguing the costs were high compared with the amount of work they would be able to accomplish. One Stoke Fleming farmer was adamant about not employing women, in his opinion 'they would not even be able to hoe potatoes for dinner, and to expect a woman to use a plough is ridiculous.' Another Dartmouth farmer thought it would be an advantage to allow boys and girls to leave school at twelve years of age, particularly as some children are already kept away from

Despite the misgivings of some, women had traditionally worked on farms, although the tasks were confined to activities such as dairying. However, as labour became short, with more and more men at the Front, women began to take on heavy duties, both on the farm and in factories.

school at the age of nine. The farmers were adamant that a boy of twelve was worth two women on a farm and, at that age, he could work a pair of horses as well as a lad of fifteen years of age.

At this Annual Meeting of the Dartmouth and District Farmers it was agreed to submit a proposal to the Education Authorities advocating children should be permitted to leave school for the duration of the war at the age of twelve.[10] With reference to children legally seeking employment, Devon County Council Local Education Authority had for some years issued a Labour Certificate to permit children aged eleven to leave school to work if their teacher confirmed they had already attended a certain number of days.[11]

Within three months of the Dartmouth farmers' meeting the need to mobilise women to work on the land began to gather momentum. Ever since the outbreak of the war women involved themselves in numerous noble causes. Nurses not only tended the sick and wounded in hospitals throughout the United Kingdom, they were also doing a magnificent job in the theatres of war overseas. Women doctors assumed a new importance because of the shortage of male General Practitioners, and Suffragettes were no longer engaged in protest and wilful damage but now fully supported the war effort.

At Dartmouth in March 1916 the scheme introduced to register local women for war work was implemented. Registration took place in the Dartmouth subscription rooms. A well-organised Committee sent out representatives to visit every household in the Borough to enlist volunteers.[12]

Dartmouth was already supplied with electricity via cable laid across the Dart from Kingswear, and any resident could be connected provided they were prepared to pay. The riverside town continued to attract summer visitors but gone were the days when moneyed people could enjoy a 12-day round-Britain cruise starting from Dartmouth, or travel from the ancient port to Gibraltar or Madeira.[13] The old three-decker sailing ship, one of the largest warships to be built of wood, and once used for training naval cadets, had come to the end of its working life and had, during 1914, been towed out of Dartmouth to be broken up. Now the cadets were trained at HMS *Britannia*, the Royal Naval College built high on the hillside at Mount Boone. Most of the Stewards employed at the college were local men, but this did not resolve the town's unemployment problem.

A source of casual employment for some men was to be taken on as 'coal lumpers', working in small gangs coaling ships that called at Dartmouth to be bunkered.[14] Many 'coal lumpers' enlisted and went off together to fight

The original HMS *Britannia*, a wooden hulk, first appeared in the estuary in 1863. She served as a training ship for naval cadets and was finally replaced by the college which opened in 1905.

Are you one of the wounded?
No Lady, merely having a Holiday.

THE INQUISITIVE ONE - "Have you
been wounded Sir?"

THE OTHER ONE - "No mi lady.
I was cleaning the canarys cage
out, an' the little beggar flew
at me."

Two Great War postcards provide a
humorous view of the plight faced
by the wounded whilst recuperat-
ing at home.

in France. As a result of the war the Naval College was enlarged, doubling
the intake of cadets, and college staff who were drafted to other naval establishment or warships were replaced by retired officers.

At the beginning of the first Dartmouth term in 1914 the cadets were told
German trawlers were in the vicinity and might open fire on Dartmouth,
consequently plans were made to evacuate the college.[15] Many Britannia
cadets, young boys aged 14–15 years old, had their college training cut short
and were, with senior cadets, sent directly to serve on a warship. This
exodus of cadets en masse resulted in local farm carts being commandeered
under DORA to transport the cadets and their bulky sea chests from the
college across on the ferry to Kingswear railway station.[16]

Whatever the official reason for sending boy cadets to war, the consequences resulted in a terrible ordeal for many of them. In the first six
months of the war it was announced in the House of Commons that 41
Dartmouth cadets had already lost their lives.[17]

The small cottage hospital, sited on the Embankment of the River Dart,
had prepared for the anticipated arrival of sick and wounded servicemen;
during the war 700 men were cared for, together with 130 merchant seamen
who were admitted after being rescued from ships that had been torpedoed.[18]

One wartime cadet was the future Lord Louis Mountbatten. Prince Louis
attended a course at the Royal Naval Engineering College, Keyham,
Plymouth, eventually joining the Devonport-manned HMS *Lion*, flagship of
Admiral Beatty.

A suspect enemy agent at Dartmouth was the focus of attention in the last
year of the war. The Royal Castle Hotel, sited opposite the boat float, was a
popular place for naval officers to stay. One of the hotel guests was arrested
and accused of spying for the Germans as he had been reported talking to
naval officers about the movement of ships, and was alleged to have passed
information on to the enemy. The accused's sister-in-law, Irish by birth, had
married a German but had been allowed to leave Germany in 1915 and
return to England. The court was in doubt about the prosecution's evidence
and the case against the accused was eventually dismissed.[19]

The growing list of casualties published in the newspapers cast a gloom over
the people of Devon but, unknown to them, the weeks ahead would bring
even worse news. The weather did not help their mood as the early weeks
of 1916 had been bitterly cold. During February Devon experienced its heav-
iest fall of snow for many years, and on the 24th of that month snow fell in

Exeter throughout the day, laying a thick carpet over the streets. A sudden thaw then melted the snow but the evening temperatures dropped creating treacherous conditions in the city.

The writer Beatrice Chase, who lived at Venton near Widecombe-in-the-Moor, describes her experience of going to bed one night not suspecting anything unusual about the weather, but on looking out of her bedroom window next morning she wondered if she was dreaming. The familiar landscape was unrecognisable to her. The moor and its granite tors were lost in a thick mist and a nearby road was blocked with a solid wall of snow, to a height of ten feet. Directly in front of her house the snow had piled six feet high and field gateways were buried. Her tenant farmer tied a long rope to his largest horse and drove it to-and-fro through the drifts to act as a snow plough, but no vehicle was able to travel along the roads. A brisk easterly wind drove clouds of powdered snow before it, but that eventually subsided and the sun came out. At 11am the postman, near to exhaustion, arrived three hours later than normal and, for the first time in his life, was unable to complete the delivery of the mail. The snow was so deep that outlying moorland farms and cottages were isolated for days, their inhabitants suffering severely through the lack of food. Eventually gangs of labourers arrived, working continually for three weeks to clear the roads.[20]

The war had a traumatic effect on Beatrice Chase who had, by the time the war started, already become well-known for her Dartmoor writings. It has been suggested that she lost a fiancée, killed in action, although this has now been questioned. She was an independent person, deeply religious, who took up a moral crusade of chastity, inviting servicemen to dedicate themselves to living a clean life by becoming one of her White Knights. The names of the committed men were recorded on a role of honour placed on the altar of a small chapel built in her garden. There she would pray for the safe return of each of her White Knights and thousands of people responded to her call, from generals to the lower ranks. Women also decided to take the crusader's vow and were referred to as White Ladies. Although Chase was a devoted Catholic, no restrictions were imposed as to who could be accepted.[21]

Olive Katharine Parr (Beatrice Chase) at her cottage at Venton. Below: the chapel at Venton.

During the bleak winter of 1916 a real concern arose of possible Zeppelin raids on Plymouth. Since the beginning of 1915, the East Coast of England and London had been raided by the giant enemy airships causing considerable damage to property and casualties. The spectre of the enemy over British soil severely affected the morale of the civilian population. Although far from the front line, people realised that this new aspect of warfare meant that no one was safe from enemy attack.

The Zeppelin was a sinister weapon that could fly over England unheeded, its silent presence creating a climate of terror. Weather conditions were a greater threat to the Zeppelins than the British defences whose anti-aircraft defences were woefully inadequate, whilst night flying for RNAS pilots was extremely hazardous.

Many people moved away from vulnerable areas and it was at this time that Devon received one of its first ever wartime civilian evacuees, a Mr J. W. Pariel from London, who came to stay at Oldborough, Morchard Bishop, seeking refuge from the Zeppelin raids.[22]

Early in January 1916, nine naval Zeppelins crossed the North Sea heading for the Midlands. Zeppelin L14 penetrated as far west as Shrewsbury creating widespread panic among the civilian population who, as a result, demanded to know what measures were being taken to combat the Zeppelins. The government, after some hesitation, authorised a chain of defences comprising searchlights and fighter stations linked to control

The vast size of Zeppelin airships is amply demonstrated by this remarkable photograph. This craft had to force land in France, drawing large and inquisitive crowds.

centres, extending from the South Coast to Edinburgh. At Devonport the Commander in Chief, Southern Command, proposed a committee be formed comprising the Garrison Commander, the Plymouth Town Clerk and representatives of the gas and electric light companies, to consider arrangements to blackout the town and nearby communities of St Budeaux, Saltash and Torpoint, if the need arose. The C-in-C, in a confidential letter, referred to the fact that Plymouth is nearer Ostend than Newcastle, which Zeppelins had already attacked, and now came the disturbing news that Zeppelins had flown as far west as Bristol.[23]

Plymouth townspeople had been advised the previous year what action they should take if the town was subjected to an air raid. Early in February 1916 a night exercise over Plymouth was planned to test these defences against an enemy attack. The alarm sounded at midnight indicated by series of short blasts from a variety of sirens and whistles, and guns were fired at ten-second intervals. The public were warned not to rush out into the street and all traffic would be required to stop when the lights went out, with horses to be unharnessed from carriages and carts. Switching off the electric light at the power station had been arranged but the problem remained how to extinguish the gas lamps in the streets.

Secret Admiralty files of Devonport Command reveal intelligence reports were collated reporting the presence of unidentified aircraft within the Command's operational area. The problem was that the reported aircraft had disappeared before anything practical could be done to investigate their presence.

On the last day of February 1916 alarm signals were sounded when Devonport received a telegram from Dartmouth Coastguard that Zeppelins had been sited heading west. The message was taken very seriously and an order went out that the light on the Plymouth Breakwater should be put out and a signal sent to a patrol destroyer to sail to the Eddystone lighthouse with orders for it to extinguish its light. The Dartmouth report turned out to be a case of a British airship failing to report its identity in the area.[24] Concern over the presence of Zeppelins in the South West continued, with many reported sightings received, often cases of mistaken identity.

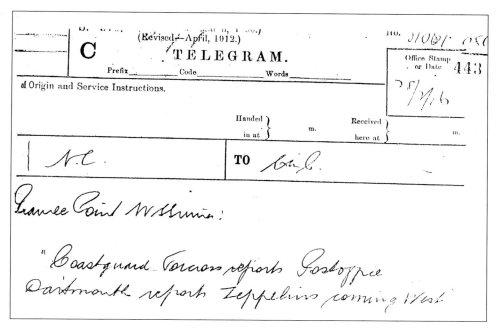

The telegram dated 28 February 1916 sent by Dartmouth Coastguard to Devonport Command warning of the approach of Zeppelins heading towards Plymouth.

The Zeppelin scare resulted in the Rear Admiral commanding HMS *Brittania*, Dartmouth to publish air raid precautions for the town. One instruction, relating to enemy aircraft approaching Dartmouth, was for the bells of St Saviour's church to be rung continuously for three minutes as a signal for the townspeople to extinguish their lights.[25]

Throughout Devon air precautions, although rudimentary, were expected to be taken seriously and an order under DORA empowered naval and military authorities at any defended harbour to extinguish all visible lights during specific hours. Later the Home Secretary issued orders for the dimming and extinguishing of lights in specific areas but the situation on lighting restrictions became so confused that it led to the Home Office becoming totally responsible for the blackout. When, in February 1916, it was accepted the whole of the country was liable to air attack, the Home Air Defence was transferred to the Army.[26]

Prosecutions were made for contravening the Control of Light Order, and a Kingswear resident living at Brookhill was summoned at Brixham Police court for showing an unobscured light, seen and reported by the Coastguard Watch.[27]

Although German policy had been to develop airships in preference to bomber aircraft, as the war progressed, and the airship became vulnerable to fighter aircraft, they deployed their giant Gotha bombers to attack England.

Trade was good at Torquay, it was Whitsuntide and many visitors had arrived at the resort. The theatre was doing particularly well, with a forthcoming attraction being advertised – Griffiths' masterpiece 'The Birth of a Nation'. This epic silent film would be screened accompanied by a 36-piece orchestra instead of the usual piano music.

Torquay Golf Club had been told by the War Department to shorten the distance of its course and to grow more hay. The Town Council was upset as they had been refused a license to hold Sunday concerts at the Pavilion, but many religious groups had opposed the application, arguing it would desecrate the Sabbath. The Torquay Master Butchers were unpopular as they announced another increase in meat prices.

The Town, with all the wounded to care for, was more a hospital resort than a place for holidays. On the last day of May 1916 a hundred wounded

Open-topped cars line the road outside Torquay pavilion in May 1916 from where they were to carry convalescing troops for a day out to Brixham.

servicemen were taken by motor to Brixham to be entertained to a tea and concert. Unknown to them the biggest sea battle in history was being fought that afternoon off the coast of Jutland where the British Great Fleet confronted the German High Seas Fleet. Over two hundred warships were involved and although the engagement was indecisive, as regards the West Country involvement it was a disaster.

News released to the British public of the great battle revealed that Admiral Jellicoe's Grand Fleet had suffered heavy losses. Three battle cruisers, armoured cruisers, a flotilla leader and seven destroyers were sunk, whereas the Germans lost 1 battle cruiser, 1 Dreadnought, 4 light cruisers and five destroyers. Over six thousand British sailors, many of them Westcountrymen, lost their lives. The first list of casualties published covered losses from the battleship HMS *Indefatigable*, a Devonport crew. A salvo of German shells had landed on her deck and there was a great explosion in the magazine before a second salvo struck the battleship. *Indefatigable* blew

HMS *Indefatigable* sank with the loss of over 1000 men at the Battle of Jutland.

Admiral Beatty's flagship at the Battle of Jutland, HMS *Lion*, built and manned from Devonport.

up and vanished with a loss of a 1000 men, only eighteen of the crew surviving. The flagship of Admiral Arbuthnot, HMS *Defence*, yet another Devonport-manned cruiser, was destroyed by gunfire and disappeared in flames. Not one member of the crew of over 900 men survived.

Devonport warship HMS *Warrior* was hit by a 12-inch shell, causing considerably damaged, and claiming 107 casualties. The *Warrior*, now crippled, was taken in tow by HMS *Engadine*, but in heavy seas was abandoned and sank. The destroyer HMS *Nomad*, sailing with a Devonport crew, was also sunk, 84 of her crew being rescued from the sea by the Germans and taken as prisoners-of-war.

Admiral Beatty's flagship HMS *Lion*, built in Devonport and crewed largely by local men, was hit by many shells. One of the *Lion*'s gun turrets was struck by a shell igniting cordite charges. The *Lion* escaped the fate of other warships by the prompt action of an officer of the Royal Marines who ordered that the magazines be flooded. He was awarded the Victoria Cross, but died of his wounds. Although the ship was saved, men in the magazines were all drowned, trapped by the action of the flooding.

With hindsight the lesson that should have been learned from the Battle of Jutland, regarding a lack of sufficient armour protection on British warships, went unheeded. The Devonport-built battle cruiser HMS *Hood*, completed after the Great War, was sunk in 1941 when a long-range shell fired by the *Bismark* penetrated her inadequate armour and all but three of the ship's crew of 1419 perished.

Among the list of warships awarded battle honours at Jutland were ten Devonport-built ships. These were HMS *Dublin*, HMS *Lion*, HMS *Minotaur*, HMS *New Zealand*, HMS *Temeraire*, HMS *Thunderer*, HMS *Tiger*, HMS *Valiant*, HMS *Vanguard*, and HMS *Warspite*.[28] HMS *Barham*, severely damaged at Jutland was taken to Devonport to be repaired.

Three days after the dreadful news of Jutland came more bad news for the nation when it was announced that Lord Kitchener had been drowned when HMS *Hampshire*, on which ship he was bound for Russia, was sunk by a mine off the Orkney Islands.

The concern of the Admiralty at the loss of the three Cressy class cruisers in September 1914 and the sinking of HMS *Formidable* was heightened by the Germans stepping up their submarine campaign. This brought the war

Airship C9 in trouble at Mullion.

closer to the shores of Devon and resulted in the establishment of a number of RNAS airship stations at various points along the coast. In the summer of 1916 an airship base opened at Cury, near the small Cornish village of Mullion. This became an important centre for anti-submarine operations, with the first airship to go on an operational patrol on 1 July 1916. This was a Coastal Class airship, C9, that had been delivered by train shortly before. Airship, C8, had earlier crashed off Start Point in Devon, killing three members of the crew. Three weeks later C9 came down into the sea at Mullion.

The Admiralty at this period chose non-rigid airships for escort duties in the Channel shipping lanes, searching for U-boats and for detecting floating mines. Both the Germans and the British had laid mines in the English Channel and there was an extensive minefield laid by the British off the coast by Dartmouth. Airships were at this time preferred to aircraft for anti-submarine operations as they were able to fly greater distances, being able to sustain flights up to four hours duration, later increased to twelve hours. Furthermore airships, unlike aeroplanes, were able to move slowly and at low altitude and, weather permitting, could even remain stationary in the air. Another advantage of airships was that they could accommodate two or more crew in the gondola suspended under the airship, whereas many early military aircraft were single-seaters. Finally, in an age when engine failures were common, an airship could remain aloft, albeit at the mercy of the wind.

Life for the semi-rigid airship crew was difficult and uncomfortable, exposed in an open cockpit for long periods of time. The pilot sat with his

Channel convoys such as this were in constant danger from submarine attack. Plymouth was one of the ports of assembly for outbound convoys composed of faster ships but aerial cover was important if U-boats were to be kept at bay.

crew in a modified aeroplane fuselage slung beneath the gas-filled bag and courage was needed to fly these lighter-than-air machines above the sea.

A most remarkable airship incident, culminating in it crashing in Devon, started on 15 September 1916, when airship SS42, broke away as it attempted to land at Milton, South Wales. The engine stopped, the undercar smashed, almost turning upside down, causing the wireless operator to fall out. Pilot Officer E. F. Monk clung on as the SS42 rose up into the air and drifted across the Bristol Channel, passing over Lundy Island. The airship then drifted inland and passed over Devon at a height of 7000 feet, when the forward starboard suspension, supporting the main weight of the engine, snapped, and the carriage and Monk swung vertically downwards to hang beneath the rest of the craft. Three hours after being airborne the SS42 began to loose height, increasing its speed over the Devon countryside, finally crashing in a field near Ermington. Pilot Officer Monk had the good sense to let go of his hold and jump clear before the SS42 hit the ground, although he damaged his back and was admitted to hospital he eventually recovered and was able to return to duty.

Pilot Officer Monk who stayed with his craft during its meandering flight across Devon.

First on the scene of the crash was Mr Edmonds of Hyde Park Road, Plymouth, who happened to be passing. Edmonds gave valuable assistance, first by sending a telegram to the Admiralty at Devonport, and then by helping to secure what remained of the airship to a tree. This was made possible with the aid of Mr Pedrick of Sexton Farm who supplied a rope and the assistance of thirty villagers from Ermington. These people were later thanked for their help by the Vice-Admiral of Devonport who wrote to Colonel Mildmay of Flete.

News of the airship crash quickly spread through the area and people flocked to the site to see what had happened. Eventually a police sergeant and three constables arriving to control the crowd. The SS42 had crashed carrying a 16lb bomb, but this was safely recovered, and someone stole the airship's pennant but this was eventually located by the police.[29]

On 1 July 1916, as airship C9 was making its first operational anti-submarine patrol from Mullion, events were taking place on the Western Front that were forever to leave a stain on the military history of Britain. This was the first day of the Battle of the Somme. Through inept planning the flower of the British Army threw itself against well-prepared defences in a futile attempt to gain new ground.

In the Devon sunshine farmers were busy haymaking. At Instow in the north of the county a large number of visitors arrived to help with this work. Strawberry teas were being sold at Mill House Weare Giffard. People in Torrington were complaining about the number of touring cars on the road and the Torrington tribunal sat to consider applications from men wanting exemption from military service. The *Western Express* reported 'Very favourable war news continues to come'.

Along the valley of the Somme river in northern France the lifeblood of thousands of men was draining into the white chalk of Picardy. What became known as the Battle of the Somme actually consisted of a number of battles that began when the first attack was mounted 1 July, the final attack being on 13 November 1916. The British, their morale high, attacked every enemy entrenched position in the area of the Somme after British artillery had for seven days pounded the German front line – a massive barrage of 1.7 million shells. Detonating powerful mines beneath the German defences,

Ten minutes before zero hour a mine is detonated beneath Hawthorne redoubt, heralding the Battle of the Somme.

British infantry came out of their trenches over the top in their thousands, advancing shoulder to shoulder in a line 14 miles long, across no man's land.

The British High Command believed the continuous heavy shelling of the enemy's position would destroy their defences, but the Germans had prepared deep underground shelters protecting them from the exploding British shells. As the infantry moved nearer to the enemy trenches, what was more a linear fortress hardly visible at ground level, the Germans appeared from their shelters, set up their machine guns, and began firing. On this hot summer's day, a day that in Devon would be called 'a day given', was in fact 'a day taken' as the British suffered 60 000 casualties, the bloodiest day in the history of the British Army. By the end of the fighting, in November, the British had advanced a few hundred yards at a cost of 400 000 men.

The mass attacks of the British at the Battle of the Somme included men from the 2nd, 8th, and 9th Battalions of the Devonshire Regiment. The following text provides no more than snapshots of their involvement in the carnage, and the trials they underwent.

A and B Companies of the 2nd Devons were part of the 23rd Infantry Brigade of the 8th Division who assembled in their trenches on 30 June 1916, their objective to capture Pozieres. After the artillery barrage had stopped the 2nd Devons, in extended line, advanced into no man's land. The following wave of troops then filed into the trenches vacated by the 2nd Devons. Looking over the parapet the troops observed the leading wave of Devons lying on the ground as if waiting for an opportunity to move forward, but what they thought were men sheltering troops was 443 dead and wounded men of the 2nd Devons, mown down by the German machine guns.[30] Private Cyril Jose of the 2nd Devons, 17 years old, recalls being out in no man's land as 'men went down like corn before a scythe'. Jose was hit in the shoulder by a bullet twenty yards from the enemy lines.

The 8th and 9th Battalions of the Devons were part of the 7th Division that went into action on 1 July. At the end of the day a roll call was made of what remained of the 8th and 9th. The Battalions had lost 463 men out of a total

Pozieres was the objective of sections of the 2nd Devon on the first day of the Somme. Here troops pass a battered German pillbox, known as Gibraltar, much later in the battle.

of 775 that had been present eleven hours earlier at zero hour.[31] Among the dead of the 9th Devons was the poet Lieutenant William Hodges, hit by bullets from a machine gun.

The Devons had begun their attack with three full-strength battalions, twelve hours later the equivalent of one full Battalion of Devons had been eliminated. The 8th Battalion remained in line, but on 3 July they spent the next two days burying the dead. The Rev E. C. Crosse, Chaplain of the 8th Devons, consecrated ground that had been the Battalion's front line trench at Mansell Copse where 160 men of the Devonshire Regiment fell on the first day. A special service was held and a wooden cross was erected over the in-filled trench to mark the grave. On it was written 'The Devonshires held this trench; the Devonshires hold it still.' A stone memorial bearing the same inscription later replaced the wooden cross and was unveiled by HRH The Duke of Kent, Colonel-in-Chief of the Devonshire and Dorset Regiment.

British troops advance into no man's land during the Battle for the Somme.

Above: German prisoners carry a wounded British soldier from a battered trench following one of the engagements on the Somme.
Below: British troops preparing to go over the top during the early days of the Somme fighting.

And so the fruitless fighting continued, with many more men killed or wounded. At Marlborough Wood a small cemetery was prepared to bury twelve Devons of the 8th; three officers and nine other ranks. Padre Crosse then wired off the cemetery naming it 'Westward Ho!', but a signaller who wrote the sign board preferred 'Westward Hoe.'

The 8th Battalion moved on and the Padre rejoined the 9th in Caterpillar Valley.[32] The slaughter was so dreadful and swift that letters written to family and friends in Devon were arriving daily from soldiers already dead.

The 8th and 9th Battalions were again in action during the third week of July. On the 20th the 8th Battalion moved up to the front line as part of the 20th Brigade to attack south of High Wood. Here A and C Companies suffered heavy casualties from enemy machine gun fire and friendly fire as the British shells fell short of their target. All the officers of both Companies became casualties.

News came through that Lieutenant Savill, Commander of C Company, was wounded. Private Veale went out with stretcher bearers to look for him and eventually found him lying in a cornfield 50 yards from the German line. Under enemy fire Veale manage to drag him to a shell crater then set off to obtain some water. When he returned he tried unsuccessfully to carry, then drag the officer back to the British line. Veale went back for help again and returned with two other soldiers and together they managed to move the wounded man a further fifty yards. One of the soldiers was then shot

Bringing in a wounded man from the wire. Stretcher bearers often sacrificed their own lives in an attempt to bring in the wounded in the face of enemy gunfire.

Theodore William Henry Veale VC, known as Tommy Veale, of Dartmouth.

dead and the two remaining men left Savill in a crater until dusk. Veale then returned with Padre Crosse and Duff, another soldier, but sighted a German patrol. Veale once again crossed the dangerous no man's land to get a Lewis gun, while Duff was holding off the enemy patrol with a pistol. Veale and Duff acted as a cover party allowing Padre Crosse and two soldiers to bring Savill back to the safety of the British lines. For his conspicuous bravery, courage and determination, Private Veale, a Dartmouth man, was awarded the Victoria Cross.[33]

Later in the year Mr and Mrs Webber who also lived in Dartmouth received two letters on the same day. The first informed them that their son, William Charles of the 2nd Battalion of the Devons, had died of his wounds in France (he was awarded the Military Medal for bravery). The second conveyed the news that their youngest son John Webber had been wounded by shell fire, but had recovered and was back in the trenches. A year later John was killed fighting in France. The Webbers, of Newcomen Road, had two other sons, one also serving with in the Devons in France, the other on HMS *Tiger*.[34] The Webbers were by no means alone in the sacrifice they made, for many Devon families were to suffer the pain of loss during the bloody battles of 1916.

The shortage of labour reduced the level of unemployment in wartime Britain. People were earning higher wages on the Home Front than ever before, but the cost of living was high and not all workers shared in this prosperity. 1916 was an important year for the up-and-coming Plymouth Cooperative Society (PCS), formed in 1860. From its humble beginnings, its membership had increased during the war years to number several thousand, with a corresponding increase in sales. Now, in 1916, the PCS purchased land and property, reflecting the improvement in the lives of many of the townspeople. The annual PCS report refers to the rise in prices that had made life more difficult for some people, but the working class of Plymouth had never been so prosperous.[35] Many employees were having their pay supplemented with a war bonus.

However, some employees of the PCS were dissatisfied with their income and, at the time of bitter fighting on the Somme, the Amalgamated Union of Cooperative Employees (AUCE) served strike notices on the PCS, that would expire on 9 September 1916. This unhappy episode can be traced back to April, when the Dockers Union threatened to strike for a 3 shilling

A group of soldiers on leave in Devon showing off captured German helmets and various other pieces of equipment.

rise for their PCS members. Later the representatives of the AUCE became active in demanding a 5 shilling war bonus, but no meaningful discussions had taken place to resolve the PCS problems and this led to PCS members going on strike for ten weeks.[36]

The PCS strike was not the only dispute in Devon during the Great War. There were strikes at two of the cabinet works in Barnstaple where the shortage of male labour resulted in the factories employing women. Elsewhere in the town customers of the Barnstaple banks were now served by 'lady clerks', and the town's bakers demanded a minimum wage of £1.80p for a 54 hour working week.[37]

Early in October Corporal Veale VC returned to Dartmouth. The homecoming was a grand occasion. For the community to have one of its members awarded the highest honour for bravery created a sense of pride. Many Dartmouthians crossed the River Dart to greet their hero off the train at Kingswear station. As he was ferried across the Dart there was, by chance, a Salvation Army Band that struck up and played 'The Marseillaise'. Arriving at Dartmouth, six men of the Devonshire Regiment carried him shoulder high up the pontoon where he was cheered by crowds who lined the Embankment. From there he was taken to the Guildhall to a civic reception. The Mayor of Dartmouth congratulated Veale who in return, amidst great excitement, thanked everyone for the welcome he had received. From the Guildhall Veale was taken in a carriage to his home at Mansard Terrace where the neighbours had decorated their homes with bunting. Later he was presented with a Testimony. On the following Monday evening Lieutenant Eric Savill, the officer whose life Veale had saved, travelled from Torquay to Dartmouth to meet up with him again. Savill presented Corporal Veale with a gold watch and chain in recognition of his deed.[38]

October was the time when the Tavistock Neurological Hospital at Mount Tavy opened for the treatment of servicemen suffering from shell shock, and other specific nervous disorders. The condition of many of the men was heartbreaking but with the tender care of the staff, and occupational therapy including poultry keeping, gardening and carpentry, many men were nursed back to a normal state of mind. Others were to experience their clinical 'nightmares' for the rest of their lives.

The Tavistock Neurology unit cared for nearly a 1000 men throughout the rest of the war. Many people, including government ministers and generals, believed that these men were shirkers, putting on an act in order to avoid active service. Those who were not given treatment were often summarily dealt with at the Front. It was only in more enlightened times that medical science recognised the plight of these individuals whose mental scars often outlasted the physical suffering of wounded men.

Tragedy also came to the county on the morning of 27 October 1916 when the worst ever Devon lifeboat disaster occurred. The Salcombe lifeboat was called out by the Prawle Coastguards to assist the Plymouth schooner *Western Lass* that had gone ashore at Lannacombe Bay, near Start Point. The lifeboat was still in sight of Salcombe Estuary but because there was no means of communication the coxswain was not to know that the schooner's crew had already been saved, and their call out was in vain. Returning to Salcombe a huge wave lifted the lifeboat's stern high into the air and, with the tide on the ebb, overturned the boat and the crew were swept into the sea. Thirteen men lost their lives, only two of the crew surviving their ordeal.[39]

The Channel off the Devon coast continued to be the haunt of enemy submarines and shipping was continuously suffering U-boat attack. At Dartmouth there are graves of Swedish, Japanese and Middle Eastern people buried in the town's cemetery, victims of the U-boat war. A salvage vessel, the Royal Auxilliary *Racer*, was kept at the ready at Dartmouth to go to the aid of the stricken steamers in this area of the English Channel, and if possible bring them back to the port for repair.[40] During 1916, John Pillar of Dartmouth, skipper of the pilot boat *Mellrose*, reported sighting four U-boats in the Channel off Dartmouth harbour. A grateful British Admiralty awarded Pillar a sum of money and he gained a Mention in Dispatches for his contribution. The German submarines not only attacked warships and mercantile shipping, but smaller boats they came across in the English Channel. On 28 November 1916, the Brixham fishing fleet out in the Channel were attacked without warning by a U-boat. The enemy submarine surfaced and sank the *Amphorite* and *Provident* by gunfire, the latter vessel being the trawler that rescued survivors from HMS *Formidable* sunk of Start

Registered in Dartmouth and Brixham, the pilot boat *Mellrose* pictured on the Dart in 1915, under her skipper John Pillar. This vessel did much good work in sighting and reporting enemy submarines.

Airship SSZ-42 at Laira sub-station (Chelson Meadow) towards the end of the war. Working these airships was very labour-intensive, as shown by the 23 men attempting to secure this craft. This airship was built at Wormwood Scrubs, West London.

Point. The fishing smacks *Vulcan* and the *Clematis* were also sunk. As the Brixham fishermen took to their boats, the Germans fired on the men. The only casualty reported was a skipper's white cat, who for twelve years had been taken on fishing trips.[41]

The Mullion airship patrols made their way up the English Channel to Plymouth and back, but the distances escorting vessels beyond the Devon port was too far for the airships' capabilities. To improve the patrol radius the Admiralty decided to look for possible sites in or around Plymouth suitable for mooring three of the new types of smaller airship that were being introduced. Four places were identified as possible sites (1) the rifle range of 30 acres and a field at Admiralty Lane, Trevol, near Torpoint, East Cornwall; (2) the Brickfields, Devonport, a large grassy area belonging to the War Department – its disadvantage being close to live electric tram lines; (3) at Ernesettle to the north-west of Plymouth – later found to be unsuitable as it was prone to dangerous air currents; (4) the most suitable site, the racecourse at Chelson Meadow, next to the Saltram Park estate (although the disadvantage here was the distance from the Naval Barracks, Devonport, where the Airship Landing Party would need to be accommodated).

A proposal had been made to erect a double-bay airship shed to accommodate a C-type or twin SS ship at Prawle, but this site was found to be unsuitable.[42] The final decision was to establish an airship sub-station on the racecourse, by the River Plym, and a balloon base at Merrifield, Torpoint, where balloon sheds and store rooms were erected. RNAS personnel were to be accommodated in the hulk of HMS *Valiant* anchored in the River Tamar. Kite balloons were flown or supplied to escort vessels from Torpoint, which base also controlled the sub-station at Torquay.

The porcine-shaped kite balloons were used for observation purposes and were flown from cables up to a distance of a mile in height. The gallant 'balloonatists' stood in a basket, suspended like a large lidless laundry hamper beneath the balloon. The observer sat on a canvas slung seat. The men who went up in a kite were very vulnerable as they were not equipped with parachutes.

CHAPTER FOUR REFERENCES

1 *Western Evening Herald*, 3.2.1916.
2 *Cavalcade by Candlelight* (1950), Eric. R. Delderfield.
3 Week Book Palace Theatre, Plymouth. WDRO.
4 *The Gilded Lily* (1988), Ernest Dudley.
5 *Play Bill* (1980), Harvey Crane.
6 *The Home Fronts 1914-1918* (1972), John Williams.
7 *Ninety Years of Cinema in Plymouth* (1972), Brian Hornsey.
8 *Okehampton Gazette*, 25.2.1916.
9 Heathcoat's Day Book, Tiverton Museum.
10 *Dartmouth & South Hams Chronicle*, 14.1.1916.
11 *Devon, Within Living Memory* (1993), DFWI.
12 *Dartmouth & South Hams Chronicle*, 17.3.1916.
13 *Official Guide to Dartmouth*, c.1907.
14 *Dartmouth and its Neighbours* (1990), Ray Freeman.
15 *Mountbatten* (1985), Philip Ziegler.
16 *The Sailor's War* (1985), Peter Liddle.
17 *Dartmouth & South Hams Chronicle*, 8.3.1916.
18 *Dartmouth Cottage Hospital* (nd), Dr W. Keane.
19 *The Castle Hotel Dartmouth* (1995), Ray Freeman.
20 *The Dartmoor Window Again* (1921), Beatrice Chase.
21 *Completed Tales of My Knights and Ladies* (1919), Beatrice Chase.
22 *Book of Morchard Bishop* (1999), Jeff Kingaby.
23 ADM 131/ 92: Station Records Plymouth. PRO.
24 ADM 131/ 65: Station Records Plymouth. PRO.
25 ADM 131/ 92: Station Records Plymouth. PRO.
26 *Civil Defence* (1955), Terence O'Brien.
27 *Dartmouth & South Hams Chronicle*, 30.3.1916.
28 *Battles and Honours of the Royal Navy* (1998), David A. Thomas.
29 ADM 131/ 64: Station Records Plymouth. PRO.
30 *Epic Actions* (1997), R. W. Gould.
31 *The Bloody Eleventh* Vol.3 (1995), W. J. P .Aggett.
32 Canon E. C. Crosse. Ref80/22/ 1. IWM.
33 *The Bloody Eleventh* Vol 3 (1995), W. J. P. Aggett.
34 *Devon Family History* No55 (1990), DFHS.
35 *Plymouth People* (1982), Reg Scott.
36 *Centenary History PCS* (1960), Reg Briscoe.
37 *Barnstaple Town on the Taw* (1983), Lois Lamplugh.
38 *Dartmouth & South Hams Chronicle*, 6.10.1916.
39 *Devon Shipwrecks* (1974), Richard Lara.
40 *Dartmouth and its Neighbours* (1990), Ray Freeman.
41 *Brixham Western Guardian*, 7.12.1916.
42 AIR 1/644: Air History Branch Records. PRO.

5

1917: THE WAR OF ATTRITION

Maybe the hand of an ancient God holding a giant compass had reached down from the sky to inscribe a perfect arc three miles in diameter that forms the shoreline of Slapton beach, washed by the waters of the English Channel. This coastal area is part of the South Hams, extending from the ancient borough of Dartmouth to the outer bounds of Plymouth and across undulating hills to the southern edge of Dartmoor. To the west of Slapton stands Start Point, a beautiful but treacherous part of the coastline, where since 1836 a lighthouse has warned shipping of the perilous rocks and dangerous tides in this part of Start Bay. And, as if these natural hazards were not enough for mariners, Start Bay was a haven for marauding German U-boats.

It was here in January 1917 a disaster occurred during severe storms and gale-force winds which destroyed the village of Hallsands, close by Start Point. The destruction of Hallsands began in 1899 when vast quantities of shingle was dredged from the shore for use in building the Devonport Dockyard extension. Within three years over 602 000 tons of the beach had been removed causing irreparable damage and placing Hallsands in jeopardy as the entire foreshore changed shape.

Up to the time of the storm the villagers, and those who lived nearby at Beesands, earnt a meagre living crabbing and fishing. Prior to the tempest of 1917 only eight boats fished from Hallsands, whereas at the outbreak of the war 38 fishermen worked 18 boats. Most of the men had subsequently enlisted in the services or were on coastal watch duty.

The great storm destroyed 37 cottages, the sea completing the destruction by washing the remaining buildings away. As one contemporary newspaper reported 'at Hallsands the beach went to Devonport, the cottages went into

A little way up the coast from Hallsands, the village of Torcross was also a victim of the storm of 1917, with cottages damaged and sand piled against the walls of others.

the sea'. The inhabitants were forced to abandon the ruins of what once were their homes. The forsaken people had to wait until the early 1920s before they were offered any compensation.

The disaster followed on from Christmas 1916 that in Devon was a very sombre affair with so many men serving away from their families and friends. The conduct of the war, with the increasing use of poison gas and the mounting casualties, hardly created a climate for celebration. Life did go on, however, and there was a happy event in the New Year when local girl Alice Powell from Laira, Plymouth, married Sergeant Spencer Bent recently awarded the Victoria Cross. The wedding took place at St Andrew's Church, Plymouth.

While people were worried about the high price of food, the Government was concerned about the level of the nation's food stocks. Politicians considered ways and means of restricting individual food consumption to account for the needs of wartime. Compulsory food rationing was rejected by the Government because of the elaborate organisation required to implement a rationing scheme thereby creating further demand on civilian labour, already an acute problem. The Government's food controller (Lord Devonport) decided to embark on a policy of directly appealing to the heads of families to co-operate in reducing the consumption of food in the household. It was suggested that the average quantities per person, per week, should be: bread 4lbs or its equivalent in flour 3lbs; meat 2½ lbs; sugar ¾lb.

Sugar was in very short supply and in many restaurants a bowl would be brought to the table by the waitress who served it directly to the customer. Households were told that economy of food was necessary and being extravagant was unpatriotic. People placed red, white and blue pledge cards in their windows to indicate their support and voluntarily imposed the national scale of food rationing in their homes. The effect of this voluntary rationing would be revealed in statistical returns to the Government Food Controller.

The Government intended to take over all the large flour mills in the country. Four Devon mills that came under Government control were Exwick Mills, near Exmouth, Marsh Mills, near Plymouth, Valle Fort Mills, Plymouth, and Thorverton Mill in mid Devon. Shortages of food were manifested in long queues, acting like a magnet for people passing by. At Brixham the shortage of potatoes was describe as a famine, and unprecedented behaviour occurred at the Town Arms, Higher Brixham, when potatoes went on sale, each customer being allowed 4lbs. People pushed and shoved to get served, the older and weaker citizens standing no chance of buying any as the crowd was so unruly.[1] The lack of potatoes was due to a poor 1916 crop, but more serious were supplies of wheat. The sugar shortage caused the Government to restrict its sale and use. Jam tarts could no longer be made and sold. At Stokeinteignhead a teashop owner was fined for supplying restricted food in excess of the quantity allowed.

HOUSEHOLD PLEDGE.

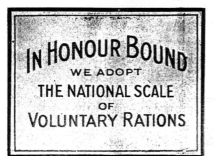

Devon Farmers had decided, or had been persuaded, to overcome their prejudice against employing women to work on the land. The Women's Land Army, formed in 1916, had been a Home Front success. In the spring of 1917 women were working on the land throughout the country. A training centre had been established in Devon where women recruits were given four weeks training before being sent out to work on a farm. A Land Girl's wage was 90p a week and they were issued with a uniform, front-buttoned

Women had traditionally done certain tasks on the farm, often associated with dairying. As with this woman, driving a hayrake on a Devon farm (*top left*), they were to prove themselves capable of any task formerly undertaken by men once the acute shortage of male labour began to have a profound effect on the supply of food. The girl on the horse (*above*) is dressed in a WLA uniform and worked for Mr Quantick who farmed at Teigngrace, Newton Abbot. A posed photograph (*left*) taken at Holsworthy c. 1917 shows three women prepared for work on the land. Although this picture caricatures the important working role played by women it contains interesting period details. That the introduction of female labour should coincide with increased mechanisation on farms is an interesting aspect of the changes wrought by war.

overalls, knickerbockers, loose fitting breeches gathered at the knee, leggings, laced boots and thick gloves. Women had also moved into other landwork, becoming skilled at cutting timber and other forestry work. Overcoming problems they faced in taking on jobs once the preserve of men, they proved themselves capable and competitive in their work. Depending on the location women in Devon were delivering milk, bread and the Royal Mail, driving horse-drawn delivery carts, and working in factories, on the railways and trams.

Sidney Prance, one-time Harbourmaster at the North Devon port of Bideford, had four sons, all serving in HM Forces. John Edward, his eldest son, born in Bideford, served in France as an Air Mechanic. Prance had been awarded the Distinguished Conduct Medal (DCM) in June 1915 for his gallantry in repairing a BE2c tractor biplane that had forced landed and was being shelled by the Germans. Prance was the first Bidefordian to be awarded the DCM. Prance, now promoted to Flight Sergeant, had trained as an Observer. In March 1917 he was temporarily transferred to No2 Squadron to accompany Pilot Officer Crossbee on a photo-reconnaissance operation over Lens. While on this mission Crossbee and Prance were shot down by the famous German Fighter Ace von Richthofen, the Red Baron, being the German pilot's twenty-second victim. Prance was wounded in the leg but

103

Baron Von Richthofen in the cockpit of his Albatross DIII surrounded by fellow members of *Jasta 11,* who together are known to have accounted for 204 Allied aircraft.

his pilot managed to bring the plane across the enemy lines to safety. Prance was taken back to England to be treated for his wounds.[2]

Five weeks later the Red Baron's fortieth kill was Lieutenant Edwin Derwin, who also lived in Devon, at Phillmore Street, Stoke, Plymouth. Derwin had volunteered to join the RFC in 1915.

Lieutenant Derwin with his gunner had flown from Savy on 11 April 1917 in a BE2c on an artillery observation mission over enemy territory, when von Richthofen suddenly appeared in an Albatross DIII, surprising the English pilot and his gunner. The Baron shot them down, the BE2c force-landing in the battle area. Both the British airmen were wounded but were able to crawl from the wrecked aircraft to an abandoned German dug out, where they were found by advancing British soldiers. Less than a month before the Armistice, Derwin aged 24 years was killed in a flying accident in a Sopwith Camel. His body was returned to Plymouth where he was buried with full military honours at Weston Mill cemetery.

After the war two other airmen who were shot down by the Red Baron came to live in Devon, Captain Oscar Grieg, shot down on 24 January 1917 lived at South Zeal, Okehampton, while Captain George Bailey, shot down on 14 February 1917, lived in his later years at Stockland, near Honiton.[3] Captain Bailey as a young man attended the same school as sub-Lieutenant R. Warneford VC

A turn for the worse in this war of attrition occurred on 1 February 1917 when Germany declared unrestricted submarine warfare against the Allies, especially targeting Britain. The German's objective was to cut essential supplies being imported into the country, their declared aim 'to bring Britain to her knees' by starving the population and severely reducing essential supplies for the production of arms.

The President of the Board of Trade reported to the War Committee that a complete breakdown in shipping would come before June 1917. The new U-boat campaign was described by the First Sea Lord as grave and serious with no solutions having yet been found to counter the menace. He told the House of Commons 'that during the first 3 weeks of January 1917, a total of 134 ships of over 100 tons had been sunk by enemy submarines'.

In that area of the English Channel immediately off the Devon Coast, shipping in the coming months would suffer increasing attacks, sustaining considerable losses. On 21 March 1917 the hospital ship *Asturias*, showing her lights and illuminated red cross, was torpedoed without warning by a U-boat five miles south of Start Point, with the loss of 35 lives, including a number of nurses. The *Asturias* had previously escaped an enemy attack on 1 February off La Havre when a torpedo fired by a submarine narrowly missed the vessel.[4]

Among the monks at Buckfast Abbey were a number of Germans. So much had public feeling turned against anyone, or anything, with a German connection that the monks themselves fell under suspicion.

Zeppelin attacks over England on the civilian population increased the anti-German feeling and even the Royal Family reacted by relinquishing all their German titles and changing their name to the House and Family of Windsor. Hatred against the Germans was so strong in the village of Buckfastleigh that a smouldering issue was raised in the House of Commons on their behalf, for a second time. This concerned the presence of forty German monks at Buckfast Abbey, all of military age. The local Urban District Council wanted them interned as enemy aliens, but the Home Secretary refused to act.[5]

People were increasingly made aware of the Government regulations they were required to observe. Careless talk was prohibited, even flying a kite was an offence as this could be used as a signal. Many were prosecuted under the Defence of the Realm Act. At Plymouth, for instance, three men were charged with having cigarettes and matches while working in a munitions factory at Devonport.[6]

As 1917 progressed meat became more scarce and food queues formed, with women and children patiently waiting to be served. In contrast hotels, although their supplies were rationed, were able to serve wholesome meals.

Many Devon towns garrisoned or billeted soldiers and local civic authorities would solicit the Army in the hope that their community would be asked to accommodate servicemen as this was very good for local trade.

Following years of prevarication and political debate at home, on 6 April 1917, the United States of America finally declared war on Germany and, near the end of the war, would begin to send her forces over to Europe to fight on the Western Front.

A major contribution on the Home Front in Devon was the collection of sphagnum moss and the preparation of moss bags for the treatment of wounded servicemen. At this period there were no adequate anti-bacterial

In the Bog

Members of Okehampton Bible Class collecting sphagnum moss.

Rakes were used to gather moss into small piles before sorting it into baskets (*right*). Then it was taken back to the depot where it was carefully dried (*below*).

agents capable of combatting infection and the few chemical substances that were available were applied as a topical treatment, for example a solution of iodine or potassium permanganate.

Soon after the war had started it became apparent to surgeons that the demand for surgical dressings would be immense. The President of the Royal College of Surgeons had in 1914 referred to 'the great prevalence of sepsis observed in the treatment of wounds,' and estimated that an average of thirty dressings would be required for each man. A note in the medical journal the *Lancet* stated that the large number of war wounds requiring dressing threatened to exhaust the nation's available supplies of material. In Britain the shortage of supplies and the cost of non-absorbent cotton and gauze, and the heavy demand for surgical dressings, resulted in experimental work to find a suitable replacement. Eventually in 1915, sphagnum moss was approved as a suitable substitute.[7]

Ironically the history of the moss as a wound dressing is credited to a German surgeon who in 1881 published a paper describing its healing

Dartmouth schoolgirls packing moss into boxes, possibly in a room at Dartmouth hospital.

properties in the treatment of wounds. The French War Department used sphagnum moss in 1895, but not until 1915 did they employ it as a standard dressing. In Britain sphagnum dressings were first used by the Royal Infirmary, Edinburgh, and its use quickly spread to England. In 1916 the British War Office officially listed sphagnum as an appropriate dressing.

Despite this recognition of the remarkable qualities of sphagnum in helping to heal wounds by keeping the lesions dry, it was not until seventy years after the Great War that researchers discovered sphagnum leaf and stalk cells are capable of absorbing liquid up to 25 times their own weight. Furthermore the absorption rate is approximately three times more rapid than cotton. In experiments in 1985 S. *papillosum* and S. *palustre* were used, although the Canadians, who sent large quantities of moss over to Britain during the Great War, refer to the quality of S. *plumesum*.[8] Pool confirms all the species mentioned above are currently growing in favourable habitat in Devon.[9] John Durant of Okehampton collected moss from Dartmoor using a long-handled rake, whilst other collectors from the town included members of the local Bible Class.[10]

The quantities of moss collected on Dartmoor resulted in the Duke of Cornwall's centre for sublimating moss opening at the former Imperial Hotel Princetown, employing 33 people. Here the moss was thoroughly dried and placed in 2oz bags, before being suspended in a heated drying room and weighed. The Prince of Wales issued the workers with a badge designed with the fleur de lis embossed in gold surrounded by a dark blue garland surmounted by a crown in red enamel and gold.

There was a moss depot at the Bedford building, Tavistock where the moss was also dried. Mary Tavy, five miles from Tavistock with a population of 700 during the Great War, also had a moss depot where Mrs Groser managed the workers. Volunteers were recruited through circulars asking individuals what they were prepared to do in helping the depot. Among those who worked at the Mary Tavy depot were messrs Collins, Ball, James, Redstone, Macintosh, Vosper, Bailly and Spies. Miss Lock was the Hon. Treasurer.

Collecting moss from the moor meant having to transport it some distance to the village. To resolve this problem Mrs Groser went in search of a donkey and cart which she purchased at Port Isaac in Cornwall, a distance of 40 miles from Mary Tavy. On her journey home people were naturally curious to see a lady driving about the country in a donkey cart. Stopping

overnight at an inn near Davidstowe the landlord, on hearing the reason for her journey, refused payment for her room and the donkey feed.

At Mary Tavy the moss was sorted and cleaned. Most of the moss was dried in the open, then taken into a shed lent by Mr Collins, and dried in the local 'Reading Room'.[11]

Sphagnum moss collectors were active in other areas of Devon including Barnstaple, Dartmouth and Torquay. At Honiton moss is known to have been collected by schoolchildren, and its moss depot produced 85 000 moss bags during the war. This depot closed in 1919.[12] At the time when the Armistice was signed in 1918 over a million bags of moss were being prepared each month throughout the country.

Princetown with its important moss depot was the focus of attention when Dartmoor Prison became a 'Work Centre' in the spring of 1917. While some convicts had been given release in order to fight for their country, they were replaced by 1200 Conscientious Objectors (COs).

The introduction of compulsory conscription brought the emotive subject of COs to the forefront of public opinion. Objectors otherwise eligible for military service were required to declare and defend their beliefs before a tribunal. The British public were strongly opposed to the COs who, with so many men in the services or about to be attested, were seen as cowards. Women in particular took pride in the number of relatives who were in the forces and to them a 'Conchie' was a disgrace. Men who objected to serving their country but who were refused exemption by a tribunal were usually sent to the Army. Those COs who then refused to wear a uniform and accept military training were harshly treated, to the extent that one group were sent to France to be executed, although the order was later rescinded.

In May 1916 the treatment of COs was slightly relaxed and an Army order was issued that they would no longer be kept in military custody but transferred to civil prisons.

The COs sent to Dartmoor Prison were accommodated in the cells, the locks having been removed. Prison warders were now referred to as 'Instructors', the Work Centre controlled by a prison governor. The Centre continued to be a place of harsh discipline; life was extremely frugal with COs given work to do inside and outside of the prison.

The forbidding granite walls of Dartmoor Prison confined many Conscientious Objectors during the Great War.

The COs confined at Dartmoor were of two groups, 'religious' and 'revolutionary', the first category having moral objections, the latter having challenged authority and circulated peace propaganda. The religious objectors represented many sects and tended to be passive. The British Israelites for instance went round trying to persuade others to prepare for the day of doom.[13] Lt-Col. Drury, the Devonport Intelligence Officer, was planted at Dartmoor in the guise of a CO in order to seek information from them, a role he found very difficult to carry out.[14]

The COs were allowed out from Dartmoor on condition they did work of national importance, and if any of them became difficult and refused to work they would be returned to the military authorities. The local Dartmoor communities were very resentful of the COs being kept at Princetown. There were even reports that the 'Conchies' diet was superior to that of civilians.

The COs started work at 7am during the week. The men who worked outside the walls were formed in groups of forty, one of their tasks being to dig the fields reclaimed from the moor. One such gang worked on Duchy land at Tor Royal. An application had been made to bring in several hundred German prisoners-of-war to assist in the construction of a roadway from Tor Royal to link up with the main road near Hexworthy, but the War Office objected.

The threat of COs being attacked by civilians and servicemen in the towns and villages meant they were forbidden to visit these places, their movements being restricted to Princetown itself. This did not prevent the COs making their presence known. Slogans were daubed on the slate roof of Princetown railway station and copies of the *No Conscription Fellowship* placed on the seats of railway carriages at the station.[15]

At Bideford, mothers and children distressed and embittered by the death of their relatives, refused to accept a CO as a teacher in the Old Town School. Most of the children had fathers or brothers on active service. The children did not like the situation and went on strike, staying away from school for three days. The teacher in question had been before a tribunal who asked that if the Germans came to his house and attacked his family would he defend them? His answer was no. The teacher left the school and went to work on a farm.[16] After the war the Bideford School Management Committee met to decide whether to reinstate the CO teacher but public opinion remained adamant and he was forced to seek work away from education.

Conscientious Objectors could retain the services of a solicitor to argue their case against being called up to serve in HM Forces. Plymouth born Isaac Foot, a well known and respected solicitor, specialised in defending COs. After the war Lady Astor contested her husband's parliamentary seat made vacant due to him having been compelled to resign the seat following the death of his father, Lord Astor, and he inheriting the title. At the election Nancy Astor was selected as the Conservative candidate, one of her political opponents being Isaac Foot who stood as a Liberal. Lady Astor won the election and became the first women to take her seat in the House of Commons. Moreover, she was American born, possessing extreme wealth, and one of the richest people in Britain, yet elected to serve a poor working-class area of Plymouth. Isaac Foot came third and it has been suggested he was unsuccessful as a result of his defence of COs.[17]

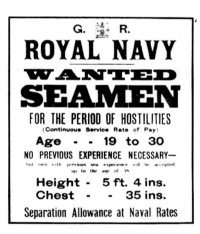

On 27 April 1917 the Admiralty decided to adopt the convoy system to protect shipping. It also assigned 44 destroyers to Devonport as a counter-measure against the U-boats.[18]

At Devonport following the departure of the Russian battleship *Tchesma*, the Russian cruiser *Askold* arrived in March 1917, and her captain requested

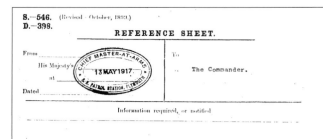

Re Behaviour of Russian Sailors on Shore.

    I beg to report that the behaviour of these men is not good.

    They appear to be able to get intoxicating liqour out of hours, as numbers have been observed under the influence of drink quite early in the evening.

    Large numbers frequent the streets that are out of bounds, also the Fancy Fair in Mill Street, Plymouth, difficulty being experienced by my patrols in clearing the approaches to this place after 10.0 p.m. (Closing time), owing to the large numbers of these men hanging about.

    They accost respectable females, complaints having been made and also requests for protection.

    The Civil Police have on several occasions drawn my attention to these men, asking whether I had any control over them.

Edward May

Chief Master-at-Arms

A letter from the Master of Arms at Plymouth complaining about the behaviour of Russian sailors.

permission for his crew to have shore leave. He believed it was essential his men should be given more liberty because of the revolutionary climate in Russia. The sailors were granted shore leave in Plymouth despite the chances of upsetting the townspeople who were suspicious of the 'Red' sailors. Later, in 1918, the first member of the Royal Navy to be awarded the Victoria Cross went to Russia and served as a lieutenant-commander on the cruiser *Askold*.

Important changes were introduced on 3 April 1917 when each air station in the South Western Group was made a separate command, with their headquarters at Devonport, under the naval Commander-in-Chief, Plymouth. Routine patrols by airships, seaplanes, and aeroplanes were introduced to cover the vulnerable areas. Special seaplane patrols, working in co-operation with destroyers and motor launches, were also organised.

    The unrestricted U-boat campaign began with the loss of 135 allied ships in the Western Approaches during April 1917, the Germans using long-range submarines based on the Belgian coast. It was at this time off Start Point that the *Medina* was sunk (see page 24).

Early in 1917 the Admiralty decided to open seaplane stations and airfields in the South West of England. These were early days regarding the use of aircraft for marine warfare, as it was only six years before that the first seaplane, an Avro D piloted by a Royal Navy commander, was successfully flown in England. In 1912 the Royal Navy possessed only three hydroplanes.

    A RNAS station built in the South West was on the small peninsula of Mount Batten, Plymouth, overlooking the sheltered waters of the historic Cattewater, estuary of the River Plym. Aircraft historian Dennis Teague refers to seaplane trials taking place in the area as early as 1913, with a small site allocated for aircraft maintenance.[19]

    The military aspect of Mount Batten is characterised by a small seventeenth-century gun tower that stands on a rocky point overlooking the

One of the earliest known photographs showing the development of Mount Batten in 1917. In contrast to the modern urbanised landscape the picture gives some idea of how barren this area once was. Before RNAS use it was an army camp

Construction taking place on one of the giant hangers at Mount Batten, 1917. Just visible behind the structure is a Curtiss Large America flying boat.

Cattewater. It was here that part of the English fleet lay at anchor before sailing out into the English Channel to confront the Spanish Armada. In more recent times the area was a popular venue for Plymouthians who arrived by ferry to relax and enjoy themselves on Mount Batten's secluded beach.

Construction work on the Mount Batten station began in 1916 and four seaplane hangers were erected, two of which are still in use for marine work. Workshops were built, slipways made, and huts erected to accommodate the ranks. The officers were billeted in a row of coastguard cottages overlooking Plymouth Sound, and the Castle Inn, facing the Cattewater, became the residence of the Commanding Officer of the station, to be known in later years as RAF Mount Batten. The public, much to their annoyance, were now barred from one of their favourite beaches.

RNAS Cattewater became operational in March 1917 and so began an interesting and proud history of the RNAS–RAF association at Mount Batten. Here twelve years' later one of the heroes of the Great War, and leader of the Arab Revolt, Lawrence of Arabia, was stationed for four years. In the Second World War giant Sunderland flying boats of Coastal Command flew out on their extensive escort and anti-submarine patrols from Plymouth.

RNAS Mount Batten 1917. The two large hangers have been completed, surrounded by station buildings. In the background, centre left, can be seen the old artillery tower overlooking the Cattewater.

Prior to RNAS Cattewater becoming operational the occasional aircraft could be seen sweeping in to alight on the water. For example on 27 February 1917 a Curtiss H8 (8656) Large America biplane flying boat arrived on transit to Tresco, Scilly Isles.

The RNAS aircraft used in Devon during the Great War were biplanes, the aircraft referred to by the name of the manufacturer and the placement of the engine and propeller. Throughout the war the Short 184 type tractor biplane, with a wing span of 63 feet, was the dominant aircraft based at RNAS Cattewater. At least 75 Short 184s at different times were based here, or were in transit.[20] This aircraft was the first to sink an enemy ship with a torpedo, this during operations on 12 August 1915 off the Dardanelles.

At RNAS Cattewater the 184s were hoisted in and out of the water by a steam crane, traversing along a metal track laid out along the Mount Batten breakwater. Official records indicate a number of the Cattewater 184s experienced engine failure and crashed into the sea, and one such aircraft,

Short 184s lined up on the break-water at RNAS Mount Batten c.1917.

The steam crane lifts an aircraft from the water.

N1636, crashed into an American ship when attempting to land at Whitsand on the Cornish side of Plymouth Sound.

On 16 November Short 184 N1257, out on patrol over the English Channel the day after it was delivered to RNAS Cattewater, attacked a German submarine with two bombs 13 miles south-west of Bolt Head.

A bizarre official report concerning a Cattewater 184 is that of a pilot sighting what at first he believed was a U-boat off Prawle Point. It was in fact a whale breaking surface, but by the time the pilot realised his mistake he had dropped a bomb on the unfortunate creature, hitting its tail.[21]

Other types of flying boat and sea plane based at the Plymouth station during the Great War include Short 240s, the Sopwith Baby, Curtiss Large America, the Hamble Baby (a variation on the Sopwith), the Wright converted Norman Thompson, the Small America, and the Felixstowe F3 flying boat – the latter looking like a giant mosquito floating on the water.

The anti-submarine airship and seaplane operations in the South West were often restricted by adverse weather conditions. In an attempt to help resolve this problem by operating from more than one base three flights of Sopwith 1½-strutter biplanes were sent to the West of England. One flight was allocated to Prawle airfield, opened in April 1917. This small RNAS station covering an area of 50 acres had four canvas-covered Bessoneaux hangers, while the men were accommodated in huts or tents. RNAS Prawle was situated close to the village of East Prawle, a remote part of South Hams. To visit the nearest town, Kingsbridge, seven miles from Prawle, meant travelling along narrow unlit country lanes, closed in by very high hedgerows. Except for the village inn, there was no entertainment available for the airmen apart from a YMCA hut. The camp Padre would send out appeals to people to donate indoor games and magazines for the 179 men who were based there, and the station lived up to its name 'Lonely Prawle'.[22]

RNAS Prawle was the first airfield established in South West England for land planes. Sited near to Start Point it was close to the hunting grounds of U-boats venturing into Channel waters off the South Devon coast.

The Sopwith 1½-strutter although built as a two-seater fighter armed with a Lewis gun, was also produced as a single seater long range bomber carrying a fixed Vickers machine gun. Designed by Sopwith, who was also responsible for the legendary Camel fighter (credited with the destruction of more enemy aircraft in Great War than any other Allied fighter), both types of aircraft were based at RNAS Prawle. These machines were capable of achieving a maximum speed of around 100 mph but they were not the easiest aircraft to fly, being involved in numerous accidents and fatalities when flown by inexperienced pilots.

Below are details of six Sopwiths, with the date they were delivered to Prawle and the date they were involved in accidents, each within period of three months.[23]

Single Seater Bomber: type 9700
N5603 Prawle Point - 23.4.17. Completely wrecked 26.4.17.
N5604 Prawle Point - 23.4 17. Nosed dived into the sea and sank 22.6.17.

Two Seater Fighter Type 9400
N5619 Prawle Point - 11.7.17. Forced landed and damaged at Salcombe 12.7.17
N5623 Prawle Point - 24.4.17. Badly damaged 9.7.17.
N5624 Prawle Point - 11.5.17. Completely wrecked 27.7.17.
N5520 Prawle Point - 27.6.17. Damaged wing on landing. 26.6.17.

In the latter part of spring 1917, three Curtiss R2 tractor biplanes built in Toronto were delivered by lorry to Prawle, two of the aircraft fitted with bombing gear. The engines of these aircraft were noisy, quieter planes were needed for anti-submarine work, and in September they were transferred elsewhere. Prawle airfield finally closed in February 1919.

A Sunday morning in Devon made the war seem a world away. Except for the people going to worship the streets were empty. No shops opened, and there was no outside entertainment on Sunday except for an occasional

Sopwith Hamble Baby.

Short 184 on the breakwater at Mount Batten.

Felixstowe F3 No.347 of 238 Squadron was among the aircraft based at Mount Batten.

A Sopwith 1½ strutter No5624 at RNAS Prawle. This was the first aircraft type to be based there, being employed on anti-submarine operations.

Six DH9s were based at RNAS Prawle after the station was re-opened following the winter of 1917.

evening charity concert. Public houses opened briefly at midday and in the evening. If the parks remained open the children's playgrounds were closed, with the park keeper chaining up the swings and roundabouts. Through tradition or law the Sabbath was expected to be observed. Sunday-best clothes were worn even if a person did not go to church or chapel. If there was an exception to this formality it was when the seasonal weather allowed local people to saunter up and down the streets, quietly socialising and perhaps hoping to hear the local gossip. For the young beaus it was a chance to catch the eye of the girl of their fancy out walking with her parents.

Serious crime in wartime Devon was infrequent but was committed. Those found guilty of murder were usually hanged, petty infringement of the law was however dealt with leniently. For example at Dartmouth in 1917 four local boys were summoned before the magistrate and each fined 10p for playing football in the market place.[24]

That summer a Tiverton magistrate granted a licence to a hotel proprietor to cater at a farm sale on condition that no more than 5 ounces of meat and 2 ounces of bread was served to each person as, said the magistrate, country people needed educating otherwise they would eat the nation out by July. Food supplies were a sensitive subject and a letter published in the *Western Morning News* criticised four men who were constructing a pleasure garden at Okehampton when they could be better employed setting potatoes. Reference was also made to the building of a tennis court in the Dartmoor town when patriotic people were digging theirs up and planting apple trees.

The Barnstaple guardians were troubled about the number of tramps in the area, and wanted to get rid of them. Tramps had always roamed around Devon, calling at night at one of the casual wards for shelter and food. They earned their night's lodging by some form of labouring task before being released to go on their way. In order to save money, the Barnstaple authorities decided to close ten of the casual wards in North Devon and many 'gentlemen of the road' were affected by the decision.

North Devon farmers recruited Swansea schoolboys to help gather in the crops, the boys accommodated at Barnstaple Grammmar School. To help the farmers who were short of horses the Devon Agriculture Committee kept a number in reserve at their depot and would loan them to enable the farmers to plough their required quota of land to grow corn. If a farmer was short of labour the Committee might also supply a ploughman.[25]

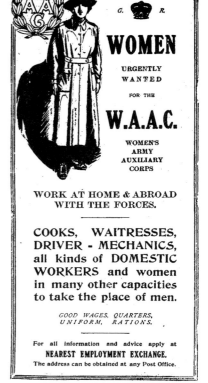

A group of women munition workers at Heathcoat's factory in Tiverton.

In the Summer of 1917 information was released that may have connections with the first time the German Army used poison gas against the British Army on the Western Front at the Battle of Loos. At the time an urgent order for a large quantity of protective cotton net had been received by the Heathcoat Textile Company, Tiverton. This normally would have taken eleven days to complete, but Heathcoat's was expected to have the order ready in 24 hours, for shipment to France. The British Army at this period were not supplied with dedicated gas respirators, and it is possible the Tiverton net was used by the British Army as one of the earliest forms of protection against enemy gas attack.[26]

More and more women were being recruited to work on farms and in factories throughout Devon, many of them facing hardship and privations brought about by long hours, poor food and bad living conditions.

Workers from Heathcoat Munitions Department in 1917. A hundred thousand shell cases were manufactured here during the Great War.

Troops marching through Torquay c.1917. The town was important both as a naval and RNAS station, and for the many military hospitals it contained.

The first contingent of disabled New Zealand soldiers arrived in Torquay as residents in the New Zealand Discharge Centres, comprising many large houses in the town. The local people sympathetically responded by organising various social activities to help them recuperate. One of the consequences of the New Zealanders' presence in the town was the significant number of marriages they made with local girls.[27]

In August 1917 an Admiralty directive stated that outward-bound convoys of ships were to assemble in designated ports. In the South West, Devonport and Falmouth were chosen, the faster ships reporting at Devonport. Three convoys sailed from the port every seven days at a speed of 10 knots. Of great risk were the ships departing from the East Coast, or the Port of London, as they were exposed to U-boat attack while making their way to the two West Country ports of assembly.[28]

Devon in 1917 was involved in many wartime activities concerning all three services. Perhaps none was so bizarre as the appearance in Plymouth Sound of a steam-powered submarine. This was a K Class submarine, built with funnels that retracted when the boat prepared to submerge. The K Class boats were a Royal Navy disaster involved in major incidents and numerous minor mishaps. One K submarine sank on her trials, three were lost in collision, a fifth disappeared completely. These submarines were the cause of many men's death and during their two years' service only one K Class boat engaged the enemy.

Devonport Dockyard constructed both K6 and K7, commissioned in June and July 1917 respectively. K6, with Dockyard workers and naval personnel on board, on her first submergence in the North Dockyard's non-tidal basin refused to surface. The situation was saved when the yard's Inspector of Engines discovered and repaired a fault in the compressed air system. Consequently the K6 rose to the surface and what could have been a disaster resulted in the Dockyard workers refusing to dive in the K6 a second time. The incident was kept secret until after the war when Inspector L. Selly, who saved the situation on the stranded K6, was awarded the OBE.[29]

The two Devonport K submarines were attached to the 12th Submarine Flotilla, assigned to anti-submarine patrols in the North Sea. This proved to be a farcical and near-tragic experience when K7 was mistaken for a U-boat and chased by the British destroyers, HMS *Observer* and HMS *Rocket*, who depth charged the K7, but somehow the submarine survived. Later the cap-

The submarine K6 was launched at Devonport in 1916. Steam-powered and fitted with retractable funnels, the K Class boats met with a succession of accidents.

tain of the K7 sighted a U-boat, fired a torpedo at it, but missed. Later the K7 fired four more torpedoes at the enemy boat, three missed and one struck the conning tower of the enemy boat but failed to explode.[30] In December 1917 the submarine flotilla moved to Rosyth where Lord Louis Mountbatten, then a 17-year-old midshipman, joined the crew of the K6.

After three years of war people in Devon became used to the number of wounded servicemen arriving in the county. It was not that they lacked sympathy but it was simply that the continuous arrival of stricken service-men became an everyday occurrence. No longer did crowds assemble out-side the hospital to watch the wounded being stretchered from the ambu-lances into the hospitals. Military hospitals large and small, including con-valescent homes, had opened in many places in Devon and men dressed in their blue uniforms were a common sight, as were limbless soldiers whose fate was to be forever reminded of the war long after it had ended.

In contrast to the presence of British servicemen in Devon there were in cer-tain places in the county prisoners-of-war. According to the Public Record Office official records of Great War prison camps in Devon have been lost. However there are records relating to German POWs in the county and in 1917, six hundred POWs are known to have been working on Devon farms, a number greater than any where else in Britain.[31]

Also in Devon eleven depots had been selected by the local Food Committees from which POWs could work. Each depot had 40–50 POWs under guard and every morning gangs of prisoners set out to work on the farms which had previously applied for their labour. After their day's work they were marched back to the depot and handed over to the guards. Individual farms were allowed to collect prisoners and the farmers were per-sonally responsible for their safe conduct.

A scheme was also introduced where prisoners were able to work and live on a farm. This category of prisoner was selected and approved by the civil police and, in 1917, eighty POWs were billeted on Devon farms. At harvest time in Devon groups of ten Germans guarded by two soldiers assisted in gathering in the crops; this arrangement also covered potato picking. Existing records indicate the prisoners conformed, there being no attempts to escape, or complaints made about their behaviour.[32]

Johann Grandyl and another German prisoner-of-war ploughing land at Denbury, near Newton Abbot c.1917.

Ella Trout who was awarded the BEM for her courage in saving a sailor's life off Start Point.

Ella Trout, 20 years of age, was daughter of the widow of a deceased crab fisherman. The Trouts had lived at Hallsands, but moved to the nearby village of Bickerton after they had been made homeless by the destruction of Hallsands early in the year. On 8 September Ella Trout and her young cousin were mackerel fishing off Start Point when an explosion occurred on a steamer that had been torpedoed and was rapidly sinking. Ella immediately lowered the sails of her boat and, taking the oars, pulled against the tide towards the sinking vessel. As she approached the scene of the incident a Salcombe boat arrived. Ella searched the water, ignoring the likely presence of the U-boat that could have surfaced. She rescued a black sailor from the water who was in a half-drowned condition, wrapping him in a sail the best she could in an attempt to keep him warm and alive. Eventually a patrol boat arrived who took the rescued sailor aboard. Of the rest of the ship's crew only nine men were alive before a boat could be lowered, and they were rescued by motor boat.

Ella Trout was awarded the British Empire Medal for her bravery and details of her courageous act are described in an official statement deposited in the Devon Record Office.[33] The parents of the sailor whose life Ella saved rewarded her with a sum of money that she used to build a hotel on the clifftop near Hallsands.[34]

On 24 September a tragic railway accident occurred at Bere Ferrers railway station a few miles north-west of Plymouth. A train carrying New Zealand troops slowed when approaching the station and a number of soldiers, thinking the train had stopped, jumped out on the wrong side into the path of an oncoming Waterloo to Plymouth express. The curve of the line made it impossible for the engine driver to see the men and the train hit the soldiers, cutting them to pieces. Nine men were killed while three injured soldiers were taken to Tavistock hospital. It was a ghastly accident with the New Zealanders ordered to go and collect up the remains of their dead comrades and take them to a nearby goods depot.[35]

The Admiralty decided to go ahead and open the Laira airship sub-station at Chelson Meadow. As there were no sheds, airships were moored to any available tree. Laira station was served by around twenty airmen accommodated in the racecourse stand where they slept on hard benches. A local boy

Wounded soldiers at Tavistock Hospital. This was the hospital to which the New Zealand troops were taken following the horrific train accident at Bere Ferrers in 1917.

A sea scout airship SSZ14 which, following engine failure, was blown across the Channel to land in France in September 1917.

records seeing the silver envelopes of the airships rising above or disappearing behind the trees as they departed or returned from their mission.[36]

Two Sea Scout Class (SS) non-rigid airships were moored at Laira. These small craft were specifically built to search for submarines in coastal waters, providing air cover that the current RNAS aircraft could not offer because of their limits of endurance. The SS Class airships were able to fly for eight hours with a small bomb load at a maximum speed of 50mph. The crew of two were accommodated in the suspended car, the telegraph operator-observer in the front seat, the pilot in the rear.

The Laira airships were a common sight over part of the South Hams when out on their patrols. Among the mishaps was the engine failure of SS14, stationed at Laira, ballooning over the English Channel and landing in France. She was later retrieved and returned to RNAS Kingsnorth to be rebuilt.[37] Later in October SSZ14 from Laira also experienced engine failure and drifted for 300 miles across to France, landing in the trenches at Montreivil.[38]

In March 1918 yet another airship associated with Laira came to grief. The SSE2, built at Mullion, and known as the Mullion twin, powered by two Rolls-Royce engines, experienced difficulties attempting to land in a gusty wind at Laira sub-station. Although close to the ground the force of the wind made the airship unmanageable. When the keel of the SSE2 was five feet from the ground the airship began to rise and all but one of the ground party that were hanging on let go. A dangerous situation developed as a cable started to wind round the neck of the airman-fitter still holding on some 500 feet above the ground. Everyone watching expected him to be decapitated but fortunately the airship crew lowered a length of rope over the side and hauled the fitter into the car. The airship, now damaged and losing gas, came down in the Cattewater about 30 yards from the south bank. At the time of the descent the tide was ebbing but the car of the SSE2, although landing in the mud, began to sink (see page 123). The groundstaff arrived on the scene and with the help of long planks of woods rescued the men. Eventually the two-ton envelope and car were brought ashore. The four men rescued were unhurt although suffering the effects of petrol fumes.

The Commanding Officer of Laira Station, as a form of recognition of the efforts of the ground crew, provided unrestricted tots of grog, an extremely rare occurrence.[39]

In France the third battle of Ypres, more commonly referred to as Passchendaele, resulted in the capture of this ruined village, a significant victory won at the cost of 60 000 British and Empire casualties. To fight a

German troops rescue a wounded British soldier from the mud at Passchendaele

determined enemy was terrible enough but at Passchendaele the rains came and turned the battlefield into a dangerous waterlogged mass, creating the most horrific and atrocious conditions for any man to fight in. The appalling loss of life was caused not only by enemy bullets but by men being engulfed in the morass of mud. To lose one's footing so easily meant death.

Repeated attacks were repulsed by the Germans who then counter-attacked. Small areas of ground were won, then lost. Undeterred by the failures and casualties the British Generals continued their attack. On one section of the Front the Somerset Light Infantry and 8th Lincolns attacked on 4 October 1917 to capture the crest of the 'Tower Hamlets' spur. As they approached their objective the Germans came forward with specially trained bombers who almost wiped out the British-held posts. The fighting became desperate as the troops were met with machine gun fire and grenades, those who survived taking refuge shell craters and attempting to make their way back to the British lines.

Trapped in one shell hole were eight men including Private Sage, a Tiverton man, married with four children. Private Sage already blinded in one eye and suffering great pain, rested his body the best he could against the inside wall of the crater. German soldiers lay outside the crater ready to attack and a sergeant trapped along with Sage decided action must be taken. In the act of throwing a hand grenade the sergeant was shot dead and the live grenade fell on his body. Sage, realising the immediate danger to everyone in the shell hole, smothered the grenade with his body in order to protect the rest of the men. When the grenade exploded Private Sage was hurled across the crater but miraculously survived, even though shrapnel was embedded in his body. Though grievously wounded he dragged himself back to the Allied lines.

Private T. H. Sage was awarded the Victoria Cross for his outstanding bravery and was being treated for his wounds at Horton Cross Hospital, Epsom, when the *London Gazette* announced his award. Before the war Thomas Sage was one of 37 men employed at a Tiverton brewery Starkey, Knights & Fords. He volunteered to join the Army in December 1914, enlisting in the

British troops crossing water-filled craters through the shattered remains of Chateau Wood during the Battle of Passchendaele.

Devonshire Regiment but was later transferred to the Somerset Light Infantry.

Early in February 1918 the London Tivertonians honoured Sage, presenting him with an illuminated address. A month later he came home to Tiverton to a hero's welcome. The townspeople hung out the flags, and crowds arrived in the town in their thousands to cheer him and, if possible, shake his hand.[40]

November was the start of a bitter winter, although there was hardly any snowfall, at least not on Dartmoor until the following April. Beatrice Chase writes of how the wind and frost combined causing the temperature to fall and killing much of the moorland foliage. Even the gorse was affected and men walked out on the moor to burn the stricken gorse, hoping if possible to save the roots. One of Beatrice's servants walked across to a nearby farm wearing an apron splashed with water after washing up the breakfast crockery and when she returned her apron had frozen stiff.[41]

The thought of a German U-boat passing through the Straits of Dover at the beginning of the war seemed unbelievable but it happened. Whatever the protection given to shipping by a naval presence, vessels continued to be sunk by U-boats, either by torpedo or gunfire. As more guns became available, merchant vessels were armed, but the chance of sinking an enemy submarine was negligible. The idea of arming merchant ships with concealed guns carrying a specially trained crew adequate to destroy a submarine was accepted by the Admiralty. The key to success for this brainwave was for the ship to be of an innocent appearance.

Over 180 vessels were fitted out for this role and were referred to as Decoy ships or special service ships. However, due to the secrecy surrounding their fitting out they also became known as Mystery Ships. When in the dockyard or port, no one except those on duty was allowed on the vessel. Among the

The Flower-class Q-ship *Pelargonium* here disguised in dazzle paint, a device developed during the Great War to confuse submarine captains as to the identity of a vessel and even the course it was sailing.

vessels used for this work special was the Brixham smack *Strumbles* M135, sunk by U65 off the Welsh coast, and the three-masted schooner *Result* Q23, once owned by Clark's of Barnstaple. At the end of 1916 the Admiralty assigned these ships with Q numbers, and the name Q-ship has since become entrenched in British naval history.

The legendary actions of the Q-ships commanded by Commodore Gordon Campbell, VC and triple DSO holder, are very much part of the history of Devon in the Great War, as most of his boats were converted and fitted out at Devonport using various methods of deception to conceal their true purpose.[42] It was very much a clandestine life for Campbell and his engineer officer. Wearing civilian clothes they would meet at a shipping office on Plymouth's Barbican to discuss their plans so not to attract any suspicion.

Campbell had selected his crew before realising not one of them had ever steered a ship. A chance meeting at Devonport Barracks with Jack Orr led Campbell to ask him if he had ever taken the helm of a ship and, on confirming he had, was immediately recruited for the job. Orr had served on the ill-fated *Titanic* and he also served as Campbell's personal servant.

Whenever Campbell's ship was at Devonport he ordered his crew to wear civilian clothes as this made them immune from the ever-vigilant naval patrols out on the streets. However civilian clothes were a disadvantage insofar as local girls would not been seen with any young man out of uniform. Later his crewmen were given permission to wear Dockyard badges 'On War Service' as some of them had been handed white feathers by women, a token that the man was a coward.

HMS *Farnborough* (QS) was deliberately exposed to an enemy torpedo by Campbell to enable his crew to sink U83. For this action he was awarded the VC, with decorations for the rest of his crew. In June 1917 Campbell was sailing, again in a disguised tramp steamer, SS *Villoria*, fitted out at Devonport Dockyard under the name of (HMS) *Parquest*. While some of the crew, the 'panic party', abandoned the *Parquest* in order to lure the U-boat closer, the remaining crew opened fire and sank the enemy submarine.

After the *Parquest* was paid off at Devonport, Campbell, now promoted to Captain (eventually reaching the rank of Admiral), decided to travel to his home in Saltash. Having missed the last train he began to walk, arriving at the Devon side of Brunel's bridge spanning the River Tamar. Here he was stopped by a Plymouth Volunteer Guard and, with permission from the

Sergeant, he was escorted halfway across the bridge, then met by an escort from Saltash who saw him home.[43]

Another famous exploit involving Captain Campbell and his crew occurred on HMS *Dunraven* which sighted a surfaced U-boat. Gunfire was exchanged but the *Dunraven* was hit by a torpedo and, despite being taken in tow by HMS *Christopher,* the sea took its toll and the *Dunraven* was abandon while on course for Plymouth. During the war Cawsand Bay became a favourite place for crippled Q-ships to lay up.

By the end of 1917 there had been further reorganisation in anti-submarine operations. The coastal routes between Hartland Point, North Devon, and around to Lyme Bay were divided into nine sections. A and B sections were allotted to the Penzance Command, D and F sections to Falmouth Command, and the remainder to the Commander-in-Chief, Plymouth. Each area employed a line of war signal stations connected to the telegraphic system of the country. There were five stations in all, including Plymouth, equipped with wireless to receive and transmit signals.

The Auxilliary Patrols continued to escort shipping along specified shipping routes. A flotilla of hydrophone vessels, either motor launches or trawlers, were attached to each command to detect the presence of submarines, but this listening system was not very effective.[44] These existing measures did not prevent shipping being attacked in the English Channel and at the end of 1917 a convoy of 17 ships sailing from Falmouth was attacked, SS *Riversdale* being torpedoed off Prawle Point, and later SS *Vinovia* was also sunk.

At the end of the year the *London Gazette* announced the Royal Flying Cross had been awarded to Lieutenant J. Budd for conspicuous gallantry and devotion to duty as a leader on a long-distance bombing raid. Budd attacked ten enemy planes that were engaged with another formation of British Bombers, resulting in three German aircraft being shot down, one of them destroyed by his observer. He then succeeded in bringing his formation back without loss. Lieutenant Jim Budd lived at Okehampton.

Early in 1918 yet another balloon, SSE2, suffered a mishap, landing in the River Plym during a gale. Based at Mullion she was attempting to land at Laira.

CHAPTER FIVE REFERENCES

1 *Brixham Western Guardian*, 29.3.1917.
2 *Under the Guns of the Red Baron* (1995), Norman Franks.
3 *Under the Guns of the Red Baron* (1995), Norman Franks.
4 *British Vessels lost at Sea* (1988), Patrick Stephens.
5 *Dartmouth and South Hams Chronicle*, 20.4.1917.
6 *Illustrated Weekly News,* Plymouth, 10.2.1917.
7 *Canadian Bulletin of Medical History* Vol 4, (1989).
8 *Canadian Bulletin of Medical History* Vol 4, (1989).
9 PC: Mark Pool.
10 *Okehampton Gazette*, 30.4.1917.
11 *Through War to Peace*: SB/TAV/1914/RIC. DRO.
12 *Honiton in Old Photographs* (1992), Dr J.Yallop.
13 *The Princetown Work Centre.*(1999) A. Greenstreet, *Dartmoor Magazine*.
14 *In Many Parts* (1926), Lt-Colonel W. P. Drury.
15 *Conscientious Objectors at Princetown*, Okehampton Museum.
16 *Hooligans or Rebels* (1981), Stephen Humphries.
17 *From Plymouth to Parliament.* (1999), Karen J. Musolf.
18 *New Maritime History of Devon* (1994), M. Duff.
19 *Mountbatten Flying Base Plymouth* (1986), Dennis C. Teague.
20 *Royal Navy Aircraft: serials and units* (1992), R. Sturtivant and G. Page.
21 AIR644 17/ 122/290. PRO.
22 *Kingsbridge Gazette*, 20.9.1918.
23 *Sopwith Aircraft* (1999), M.Davis.
24 *Dartmouth & South Hams Chronicle.* 20.4.1917.
25 *North Devon Herald*, 17.5.1917.
26 *Tiverton Gazette*, 10.7.1917.
27 *The Devon Historian* (April 1996), John Pike.
28 *Submarine Campaign Seaborne Trade* V.III. Official History,
29 *K Boats* (1999), D. Everitt.
30 *K Boats* (1999), D. Everitt.
31 *Dartmouth and its Neighbours* (1990), Ray Freeman.
32 1262, M/ LH2. DRO.
33 1262, M/ M/ 6122. DRO.
34 *From the Dart to the Start* (1994), Chips Barber.
35 *The Times*, 3.10.1917.
36 *Western Morning News*, 6.12.1963.
37 *Battlebags* (1998), C. E. S. Mowthorpe.
38 *Battlebags* (1998), C. E. S. Mowthorpe.
39 *Western Evening Herald*, 8.11.1963.
40 *Passchendaele 1917* (1998), Stephen Snelling.
41 *The Dartmoor Window Again* (1921), Beatrice Chase.
42 *A Short History of Devonport Royal Dockyard* (nd), G.Dicker.
43 *My Mystery Ships* (1928), Gordon Campbell.
44 *Naval Operations Vol 5. Official History,* H. Newbolt.

6
1918: THE UNEXPECTED VICTORY

The past year had been a traumatic period. Casualty lists lengthened each month and everyone prayed the fighting would cease, but how this would come about was impossible to visualise. Gone was the early enthusiasm and few people now dared to predict when the conflict would end. The fact was the country was weary of war.

In January 1918 there was a shortage of food in Devon. Supplies of butter, margarine and cheese had disappeared from the grocer's counter. Butcher's shops at Newton Abbot closed twice a week as there was no meat to sell to the public. A rumour that a grocer in the town had a stock of margarine created near-hysteria as people pushed into the shop and crowded on to the pavement intent on obtaining a supply. Even when the grocer denied he held any stocks nobody believed him and the police had to be called to restore order. This particular Newton Abbot grocery store was regularly looted, with people stealing dried fish, biscuits and jam.[1]

Early in 1918 the Minister of Food introduced a food rationing scheme for London and the Home Counties. This was later extended throughout the country, with ration books distributed to civilians. Meat was officially on ration from April, followed by sugar, butter and margarine. Anyone breaking the rationing order were liable to be convicted.

Later, a 'Blackberry Order' was introduced prohibiting the use of this fruit except for personal consumption or for the manufacture of food. The object of the order was to secure the largest possible quantity for the jam manufacturers. If farmers did not gather the blackberries on his land a local organisation would intervene to ensure the berries were not wasted.

This postcard view of Newton Abbot, taken just after the war, reveals how important such market towns were to the surrounding community. Locally grown produce was bought and sold here and, during the Great War years, the weekly market was an essential source of food for people from a wide area.

Far away in the Dardanelles during January 1918 the Devonport-crewed submarine *E14* was lost while attempting to sink the German battlecruiser *Groeben*. The Commander on this operation Lt G. S. White was posthumously award the VC. The surviving members of the crew were taken as Turkish prisoners-of-war and their names were dropped from a German aircraft over British lines so that their fate might be known. The list included Samuel Henry Ball who was from Above Town, Dartmouth, and Seaman Bowhay who lived at Clarence Street, Devonport.[2]

DH6 B2903 of 517/18 Flight 254 Squadron based at Prawle airfield.

The Royal Air Force came into being on the 1st April 1918 with the merging of the RNAS and RFC. This resulted in the RAF in the South West being under the Command of No.9 (Operations Group), Mount Wise, Devonport. Later in the year further reorganisation created ten RAF Wings that reported to No.9 Group. In South Devon RAF Prawle Point re-opened in April where 6 Airco DH9 aircraft were delivered. The DH9, derived from the DH4, was originally designed as a two-seater reconnaissance plane, but had been used as a long-distance bomber. There were many variants of the DH9 but all suffered criticism relating to their performance.

The Prawle flight of DH9s was attached to 254 Squadron and used for anti-submarine patrols, suffering mixed fortunes. A Prawle DH9 while out over the Channel attacked a U-boat with two 230lb bombs, while D1681, two weeks after being delivered to Prawle, came down at Paignton and was completely wrecked. From July a flight of nine Airco DH6 biplanes sent to RAF Prawle met with ill-fate. Within three months five were involved in accidents, for example C5200 crashed at Gara Rock, and C6515 forced landed, then crashed by Stoke Church, near Slapton.[3]

A Short 184 being lifted on to the quayside by crane at Torquay RAF station, 1918.

RAF Torquay seaplane and kite balloon station opened on the 30 May with the formation of Flight 418. This small twelve-acre station attracted much public attention as it was sited at picturesque Torquay harbour (this same location was later used by American troops embarking for the D-Day landings in 1944). Here on Beacon Quay Bessoneaux hangers, seaplane sheds and a balloon shed were erected.[4] At least twelve Short 184 seaplanes, were based at the station, a crane hoisting the aircraft on to or out of the water. The seaplanes would take off near Haldon Pier.

Torquay was also a kite balloon sub-station for No.16 Balloon Base Merrifield, Torpoint. Dummy Balloons, that is without any observers, were fixed to local fishing trawlers when they went out to sea. In July 1918 the RAF, using the Defence of the Realm Act, compulsorily acquired land at the Old Fort, Berry Head, to establish a kite observation balloon station. Experiments were carried out with a C Class submarine based at Dartmouth to ascertain at what distance from Berry Head a submarine could keep up a diving patrol without fear of being detected.[5] East of Torquay an emergency aircraft landing ground was planned to be laid out at Exmouth.[6]

The dearth of information at The Public Records Office relating to Great War prisoner-of-war camps in Devon is no indication that low numbers existed in the county. The *Western Morning News* revealed that a number of POW camps had been opened in Devon, one being at Okehampton.[7] Sir Charles Cava of Sidbury even had a 'private' camp that employed POWs.

German prisoners were recognised as being good workers and farmers complained they were not getting their fair share of POW labour. Migratory gangs of POWs were then sent all over the county to work, for example to Budleigh, Kenn, Cheriton Bishop, Honiton, Salcombe and Tavistock.[8]

The notification of Devon servicemen and women awarded medals for gallantry and distinguished service were usually published in Devon newspapers. Understandably the spotlight was centred on those fighting or serving in one of the frontline theatres of war. However there were many acts of bravery and devotion to duty on the Home Front that were also officially recognised. On one cold day in April 1918 the Earl Fortescue, Lord Lieutenant of Devon, accompanied by the Mayor of Plymouth and a large gathering of civic and service representatives assembled on Plymouth Hoe to present medals, including one to young heroine Ella Trout of Hallsands (see previous chapter), who travelled to Plymouth to receive her British Empire Medal (BEM). Five Dockyard workers were also awarded the BEM for their work on trials in submarines. They were John Andrewartha, Thomas Cosby, Thomas Hobbs, Richard Sandhurst and William Trotman. Two men were given awards for their bravery in refloating a damaged ship that had run aground during a storm, while William Bryant received the BEM for his prompt action dealing with an explosion that occurred in a Plymouth munitions factory where 140 men were working. Robert Davies was awarded the BEM in connection with an explosion that occurred on diving operations, also during submarine trials.[9]

Gallantry was very much in evidence in April when, within ten days of each other, two Devon men were awarded the Victoria Cross. John James Crowe, born at the Garrison Hospital, Devonport, won the VC and Croix de Guerre at Neuve Eglise on 14 April 1918.[10] Richard Sandford, born at Exmouth and the second son of the Archdeacon of Exeter, was a Lieutenant in the Royal Navy's submarine service. Already holder of the Distinguished

A remarkable aerial view of RAF Torquay under construction, adjacent to Beacon Quay. Although the work is not completed there are already 3 Short 184 seaplanes on the quayside. At the bottom left hand side of the picture can be glimpsed a patrol boat.
It was here in the Second World War that concrete hards were built to convey amphibious craft on to ships for the D Day landings.

Blockships at Zeebrugge, 1918 (*above*). Captain Carpenter (*above right*), with arm in a sling, commander of the *Vindictive*, and men who took part in the Zeebrugge raid, including Royal Marines from Plymouth.

Service Order received while serving at the Dardanelles, Sandford was given Command of HM Submarine C3 in a operation to block two major ports used by the Germans.

Although the U-boat campaign continued, there had been no major naval engagement save for some operations in the Baltic. However in 1918 the British drew up plans to curtail German submarine activity from North Sea ports, Zeebrugge and Ostend. Two U-boats a day were emerging from Zeebrugge to attack Allied shipping and the objective of the operations was to prevent this. Under cover of a large naval force, assisted by landing parties who were to attack port installations, the Royal Navy were to attempt to place blockships across the narrow mouths of the harbours.

Participating in the Zeebrugge raid was the 4th Battalion of the Royal Marines who had drawn lots to see who should be first to land. C Company, all Plymouth Marines, won. On landing they were to divert the Germans while the navy attempted to seal the entrance to the Bruge canal using two old British cruisers laden with concrete. The four platoons of C Company who landed were slaughtered, only a handful of men surviving.

The naval vessel carrying the Marines into battle was HMS *Vindictive* which was to land them on the Mole, a long curved seawall linked to the land by a steel bridge. Lt Sandford had volunteered to sail the submarine C3, packed with explosives, into the bridge and blow it up, thus preventing enemy reinforcements approaching the *Vindictive*. Two submarines were originally involved in the daring, dangerous mission, but C1 was forced to turn back. Sandford however successfully reached his objective and crashed C3 into the latticework structure of the bridge. He and his crew then scrambled into a small boat having set a time-delay fuse on board C3. Under a veritable hail of small arms fire Sandford and a crewman were hit while escaping. The submarine then blew up and Sandford's daring feat was successful.

However the raid as a whole, though deemed a brilliant success at home, was costly in and men and ships, and the Germans soon had the ports reopened.

After recovering from his wounds Sandford was presented with the Victoria Cross by King George V but a few months later, on 23 November 1918, aged 27 years, Sandford died after contracting typhoid. His Victoria Cross is in safe keeping at HMS *Britannia*, the Royal Naval College, Dartmouth.[11]

Lt Richard Sandford VC.

The demand to grow more food had been tempered by the acute shortage of labour. This was not helped by public criticism of farmers' sons evading military service. In 1915, the cultivated land in Devonshire covered 1.2 million acres, of which 479 000 were arable and 729 000 in permanent grass. The quota of additional land tilled for corn in 1917 was 130 000 acres.

There were in 1918 nearly 12 000 Devon farms registered by the Agriculture Executive. The majority of these were small, worked mainly by family labour. Discord had arisen among rural Devon Parishes regarding Army recruitment, partly due to the Rural Tribunals which had a bias to the needs of agriculture.

In order to enlist more men from rural areas a policy of the 'Clean Cut' was announced and the Devon Agriculture Committee was given a quota of men they were to find. Devon, for purposes of this 'Clean Cut', was divided into 4 divisions. North Devon were to supply 278 men, South Devon 200 men, East Devon 253 men, and 219 men were to come from the west of the County. The men would be taken from the ages of 23–31 years and the Committee were expected to find 1257 men for enlistment. An investigation later revealed there were not sufficient fit men to meet the required quota.

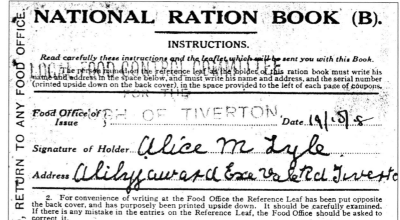

The records of the Lord Lieutenant of Devon reveal that in the North Division of the County one half of the men under proclamation were refused their appeal by the Military Tribunals. This was considerably more severe than in the other areas and in some cases the only able-bodied man, other than the tenant farmer, was taken for military service, leaving the farmer to do the best he could with perhaps a teenage lad, or any other help he could find. Many of the men in the 23–31 group could not be taken from their farms as they were the occupying tenant. Furthermore 25 per cent of this age group were declared unfit for service.

Of course there were many farming families who had already suffered the loss of their sons, killed on active service. Moreover, the low recruitment of men from the land was not simply about some being more patriotic than others. The prewar problems of farming in Devon centred on a lack of suitable cottages for labourers, on more men marrying and moving away to get their own farms or, drawn by the prospect of higher paid employment, moving to the towns and cities. Large numbers from Devon had emigrated prior to the outbreak of war.

The introduction of tractors helped mitigate the labour problem, but they were unreliable, expensive, and many fields were too small and steep to be ploughed by anything but horses.

From all this it can be seen that one of the fears faced by the county's Agriculture Committee was that more men would get out of farming leaving too few to work the land. Indeed, near the end of the war 2774 soldiers had been diverted to work on farms in Devon, with 56 ploughmen seconded from the 3rd Devon Regiment.[12]

The introduction of the convoy system had led to a significant reduction in the number of ships being sunk by U-boats and now, to reinforce the Channel patrol in the South West, a flotilla of American submarine chasers and a US destroyer arrived in Plymouth, based at the Victoria Wharves, Cattewater. Later this flotilla was increased to 36 vessels, together with USS *Aylwia*.

US sub chasers, stationed at Plymouth, off the coast of South Devon. The photograph was taken from airship SSZ27 on 20 May 1918.

Six of the US submarine chasers proceeded to Torquay for special training while more arrived at Plymouth, bring the total up to 66 craft. The chasers had a radius of up to 1200 miles and a maximum speed of 17 knots with each boat having a radio telephone system installed, enabling them to communicate up to 20 miles. The US naval officers were accommodated at Elliot Terrace on Plymouth Hoe, close to the home of the Astors.[13]

The Devonshire Regiment had been involved in various theatres of war, fighting with a gallantry not always reflected in the award of decorations. The battles of the Somme, Loos, Kut and Passchendaele are among the the places where they saw action, and to this honoured list must be added Bois des Buttes which saw one of the most heroic actions of the Great War. Situated north of Rheims, close to the River Aisne, it was here on 27 May 1918 that the 2nd Battalion of the Devonshire Regiment fought its way to glory. Under intense bombardment, cut off and with no hope of rescue, the gallant Devons fought to the last man.

Earlier, in April 1918, the Germans had launched a massive offensive on the Western Front intent on defeating the Allied armies before the introduction of American troops had a decisive effect on the balance of forces. The ferocious German attacks threatened to overrun the Allies and before the offensive came to a halt both sides had suffered huge losses, with the British 5th Army virtually destroyed.

The 2nd Devons, having been long in the line and understrength by a 100 men, were relieved by the French and moved to a rest area, in a place believed to be a quiet sector. However, facing them across no man's land were fresh German divisions and artillery brought up to the Front unnoticed. The only advance warning of an attack came from the interrogation of two German prisoners who revealed the German's would resume their offensive at 1am on 27 May. On 26 May an order was given for the Devons to be in fighting order at 8pm and at midnight they were taken to a large tunnel, sufficient to accommodate a battalion, on the side of a hill – the Bois des Buttes. On their front the 2nd West Yorks held the British Front Line, elements of the Middlesex Regiment supporting them, and in reserve the 2nd Devons, sheltering in the Bois des Buttes.

At 1am a thunderous German bombardment began with high explosive (HE) and gas shells raining down on the British positions. In the tunnels the Devons were safe from the HE shells, but the gas curtains at the tunnel entrances were ordered to be dropped. Meanwhile the Yorks and the Middlesex suffered terrible losses due to the bombardment.

On 27 May 1918 what was to become known as the Third Battle of the Aisne opened with an intense bombardment from the German guns. This howitzer is one of over six thousand artillery pieces secretly assembled before the battle.

At 3.45am the enemy's barrage lifted and was now directed to the rear areas where the British gun positions were sited. As communications had broken down a company of the 2nd Devons decided to evacuate the tunnel shelter and occupy the trenches, or what remained of them after the intense enemy shelling. But unknown to the Devons the German infantry had penetrated the British positions and were overrunning the defences. Few details exist to explain what happened, it is thought that the destruction of the trenches was partially responsible for the battle being fought in small groups by the surviving Devons. Though isolated, the intensity of the fight shown by the Devons made the Germans believe the British presence was far greater than they originally supposed and the action crucially delayed their advance. For many of the 2nd Devons however this was to be their last resting place.

Back in Devon on this hot sunny day people were expressing concern over the rising cost of train fares. The railway companies before the war would run cheap excursion to seaside resorts but now, with fewer visitors, fares had increased by fifty per cent. The editor of the *Sidmouth Gazette* wrote 'We

The final German onslaught made use of gas shells, claiming many victims. Many of these men, those who survived, would face a broken life of chronic illness.

here, have much to be thankful for, we live in clover, and we chafe at our little inconveniences, it is well to remember how splendidly we have been preserved from scenes in France'.

Indeed the Devons on this day were ordered not to retreat, to hold their ground at all costs. The written order did not reach them and, anyway, the men had been broken into small units, unable to communicate with each other. B Company was now confronted by a long line of German infantry, preceded by storm troopers. Two enemy tanks approached, each fitted with a cable flying an observation balloon assisting the enemy machine gunners and spotting British gun emplacements for the enemy to shell. No 5 and 6 platoons of B Company made three unsuccessful attempts to break off from the fighting, and eventually 6 platoon managed to get away, but 5 platoon were mown down by the machine guns while making a last stand. Those remaining finally charged with fixed bayonets but most of them were killed.

One platoon from C Company emerged from the tunnel shelter to attack the approaching enemy but, within a 100 yards, half the platoon were killed before reaching the shelter of the nearest trench. Here the remainder clung on until they were reduced to just seven men.

Against the odds the survivors of the various companies managed to link up and continued to offer stubborn resistance. Two officers and fifty men charged down a hill firing at an approaching German artillery team, those surviving then making their way back up the hill. Then, as the men prepared for what would have been a final suicidal charge, their Captain was injured and the remaining Devons overwhelmed.

The 2nd Devons were all but annihilated, a few were taken prisoner by the Germans, while remnants struggled back to the rear. What now remained of the 2nd Battalion of the Devonshire Regiment joined up with the French, repelling a number of attacks until the German advance was halted. In all the Devons lost 23 officers and 528 other ranks but their heroic action allowed the Allies to secure their defences south of the Aisne.

In recognition of their stand the 2nd Devons were the subject of a special order, the French awarding the Battalion the Croix de Guerre avec Palme.[14] Not a single man of the 2nd Battalion was awarded a medal but after the Great War their immortal stand was remembered by the county in a solemn memorial service during the month of May.

On the third day of the Battle of the Aisne, remnants of the Devons joined with French troops in order to counter the German thrust.

During the war Jewish militants had been campaigning for the establishment of a Jewish regiment to fight alongside the Allied forces. There were many young Jewish men living in England that were ineligible to serve in the British Army. Then in August 1917 the *London Gazette* announced the formation of a Jewish Regiment. The 38th and 39th Battalions of the Royal Fusiliers enlisted many American Jewish volunteers, while the 40th Royal Fusiliers accepted Palestinian Jewish volunteers. The Regiment referred to as the 'Jewish Legion' served in the Middle East fighting against the Turks. In July 1918 three Battalions of the Royal Fusiliers were stationed at Crownhill Barracks, among them David Ben-Gurion who was eventually to become the first Prime Minister of Israel. In a letter to his wife he writes that he is staying at Egg Buckland and how impressed he is by the green mountains and valleys of Dartmoor. He tells his wife how the Sabbath is observed, and how the Jewish soldiers are excused training, allowing them to march to the Synagogue in the centre of Plymouth together with the officers, led by the colonel of the regiment.

Around the Devon coast the anti-submarine patrols were extended. At Westward Ho! a small circular airfield opened in June 1918, sited on a golf course at Northam Barrows and covering an area of 90 acres. From here aircraft maintained a patrol along the North Devon coast, acting as a deterrent to U-boats. These aircraft were kept in Bessoneaux hangers, the airmen accommodated in huts, while a large wooden shed served as a mess and guardroom. In August, the DH6 aircraft stationed there were formed into No.502 and No.503 (special duty) flights.[15] In September eight Airco DH6 biplanes of 250 squadron were delivered, the first of this batch crashing on the beach south of Hartland Quay, while another on the same day suffered engine failure and came down in the sea, the pilot being rescued from a ship in a passing convoy.

The layout of RAF Westward Ho!

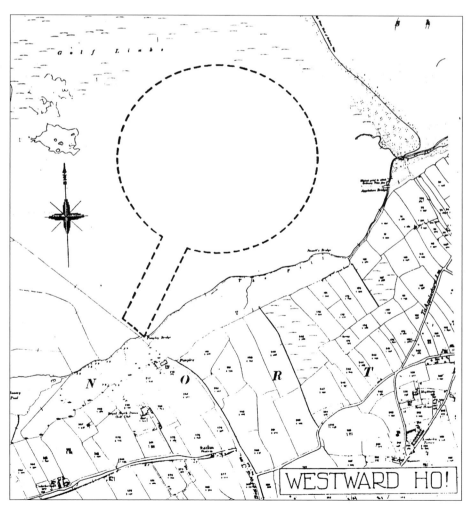

The airmen of RAF Westward Ho! formed a concert party that gained a high reputation locally. Early in September 1918 the concert party, having performed at Bideford, arranged to perform at Runnacleave Hall, Ilfracombe. However on the day of the performance bad weather prevented the airmen from advertising their show which they had intended to do by dropping handbills from an aircraft over the town![16]

A large part of Barnstaple's industry was devoted to war work. Along with the munition works, the cabinet factories were engaged in producing component parts for aircraft, while another factory contracted to make caterpillar tracks

An aerial view over Barnstaple showing the slipways on the riverside (*far right, centre*) on which the concrete barges were constructed and launched.

for the army. One company even produced large quantities of mosquito net for the troops out in Mesopotamia.

Thousands of people arrived in Barnstaple early on Saturday morning on 21 September to watch the launch of the first ferro-concrete barge, named the *Cretpath*. This was a new concept in shipbuilding created as a cheap way of replacing ships lost to U-boats in which the British Construction Company planned to produce concrete barges that could be completed in four months. At Anchor Wood, nearby Barnstaple Bridge, six berths were constructed on which the barges could be built and launched. The considerable amount of publicity leading up to the day of the 'Barum launch' resulted in the event becoming a great social occasion. The crowds thronged the streets, entertained by the band of the Devonshire Regiment. The River Taw was a mass of boats and yachts flying pennants and flags, cruising up and down the river. The *Cretpath* was launched at 7.20am but this did not deter sightseers from turning up, and after the launch the official guests were entertained to breakfast by the company in a large marquee. Later in the day 600 employees of the shipbuilder sat down to dinner in Barnstaple's Market Hall.[17] The only damper to the day's festivities was that the barge became stranded on the riverbank after the launch and, when later an attempt was made to refloat it, its back was broken in two places.

The Great War of attrition continued. Although people retained their faith in victory many were tired and shrank from the thought of more bad news from the Front. Yet there came a spectre of death beyond their worst imaginings. From the summer of 1918 through to the winter months, an unbelievable death toll mounted with the coming of the great influenza pan-

demic that swept the world killing an estimated 21 million people. Half the global population is believed to have suffered. No human infection of this magnitude had occurred since the coming of the Black Death in the fourteenth century.

Exactly where this virulent disease started is unknown but contemporary descriptions refer to it as the Spanish Flu. At the time of the pandemic very little was known about the infecting agent or any other viruses. Not until fifteen years later was the the influenza virus isolated and three groups identified: groups A, B and C. Which type caused the 1918 pandemic has so far not been confirmed, but the belief is that it was a virus related to a modified swine influenza agent.

During 1918 influenza was never entirely absent in the UK population. There were indications during the summer of that year that an epidemic had started, yet at the end of August the rate of infection subsided, although not disappearing. The summer episode of the infection was characterised by how in a perfectly healthy school this influenza strain would within hours affect a large proportion of the students to the extent that they were unable to carry on, yet within a short time their temperature was down, and the patients' felt considerably better. Convalescence was rapid and this clinical condition was referred to as 'Three Day Influenza'.

With the coming of Autumn a most virulent strain of influenza appeared that to many people was lethal. What at first appeared to be a mild case of the disease had to be regarded as potentially grave, with a poor prognosis. A patient may appear to be progressing well when suddenly the individual's condition could change for the worse, with death occurring within 24 hours due to an acute pulmonary infection. Medical care was essentially confined to nursing and the administration of various pharmaceutical preparations, but there were no effective therapeutic substances that would destroy the virus. At this period no prepared influenza vaccines were available.

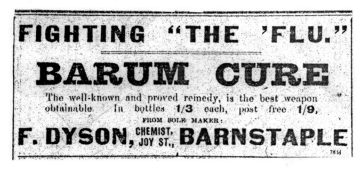

FIGHTING "THE 'FLU."

BARUM CURE

The well-known and proved remedy, is the best weapon obtainable. In bottles 1/3 each, post free 1/9.
FROM SOLE MAKER:

F. DYSON, CHEMIST, JOY ST., BARNSTAPLE

Bideford born Flight Sergeant Prance DCM had the dubious honour of being shot down by the Red Baron. Surviving this, he was to fall victim to the Spanish Flu epidemic of 1918.

The influenza pandemic swept down to and through Devon. At Bideford it caused the death of a local hero, with tragic consequences. On 16 June 1918 Second-Lieutenant John Prance, DCM, who had been shot down by the Red Baron, received a telegram with the sad news that his baby daughter had died. Prance, already suffering the symptoms of influenza, hurried back to his home in Elm Grove Bideford but en route his clinical condition rapidly deteriorated. On arrival he was so ill that he went straight to bed, unable to attend the funeral of his daughter. The following day he died. Prance was buried with full military honours in Bideford public cemetery.[18]

This dreadful story of family suffering was to be experienced by many other Devon families. At Ilfracombe Mr and Mrs Blackford, having just received news of the death of their son, killed at the Front, were further bereaved when their daughter, feeling unwell, rapidly became worse and died four days later – the cause of death, influenza.[19]

During July 1918 the Deputy Medical Officer of Health for Brixham submitted in a report 'there were a lot of people running around with the Spanish Flu Epidemic.' During the last week of October the number of cases had significantly reduced, however by the middle of November the virus had spread throughout Brixham. The Medical Officer thought that the severe cases could have been imported from outside Brixham, suggesting Devonport, where Brixham families had been travelling to stay with their relatives in the navy.

This virulent strain had a short incubation period. A working party of a hundred men from RAF Torquay stationed at the Brixham Air Station at Berry Head showed symptoms of the infection within three days of arriving. Subsequently six airmen became seriously ill and were admitted to hospital. The following day more Torquay airmen were admitted. The environment at Berry Head would have been favourable for the transmission of respiratory diseases as sixty airmen lived and slept in one large room.[20]

At Brixham Cottage Hospital the nursing and kitchen staff, with the exception of Matron and Sister, succumbed to the virus. Although there was a medical service in Brixham, home visits were not prompt, even less so at the peak of the epidemic when the District Nurse and Midwife became infected. Medical care suffered further when the maternity and child welfare centre closed down. The situation became so acute that most of the population had to fend for themselves as friends and neighbours were either too ill, or busy looking after their own relations. Preventative measures introduced to control the spread of the infection was to close all the Brixham

Military Hospital at Stonehouse (*foreground*) c. 1918. Already full of war wounded such hospitals found themselves overwhelmed by the hundreds of influenza cases.

schools and to cancel the special children performances and second house showings at the town's cinema.

During 1918 there were 25 victims of influenza in the Brixham area most of whom were women from the 25–45 age group. The town's Medical Officer believed the reason could be due the very thin stockings women were wearing, reporting that 'they go about with bare chests and other eccentricities of fashion.'[21]

From summer to early winter influenza spread throughout the county. On 25 July, 42 people died at Exeter, and 35 deaths were reported in Plymouth. Later, at Plymouth, from October to November, 432 people died from the influenza virus. These sample figures reflect the severity of the pandemic in Devon and the Medical Health Officer of the county announced 516 schools were closed, and that five teachers had died. He reported that he had received a telegram informing him 'People were dying right and left at Appledore', as there was no medical care in the town. An order was issued to get help for the townspeople even though there were insufficient doctors in North Devon. Medical facilities were so short the local workhouse was used to admit a few clinically ill patients.[22] In the third week of October the obituary list in the *North Devon Herald* had never been so long, with the names of 54 people who had died of influenza

PLYMOUTH EDUCATION AUTHORITY.

INFLUENZA EPIDEMIC: CLOSURE OF SCHOOLS.

ALL THE SCHOOLS OF THE AUTHORITY BOTH ELEMENTARY AND SECONDARY (INCLUDING EVENING SCHOOLS) WILL REMAIN CLOSED UNTIL FURTHER NOTICE. The Teachers of all the Schools, however, will be present at their respective Schools at 9.30 a.m on Monday, November 11th, in order to arrange Organised Games and Play and other Out-of-School Occupations. Parents are asked to send their children to their own schools at that time.
E. CHANDLER COOK,
Education Secretary.
Education Office, Plymouth.

In September ten American Soldiers were buried in Paignton cemetery. They had been patients at the Oldway and Redcliffe hospitals. New Zealand soldiers from Torquay acted as coffin bearers. More were buried the following day and over fifty men had died so far in the town.

Reports from Dartmouth in early November indicate the influenza outbreak in the town was very severe. Schools were closed and all social functions postponed. Dartmouth Corporation considered reopening the town's soup kitchen to ensure invalids had sufficient nourishment. On 1 November eight deaths were reported, ten days later another thirteen people died. There were several deaths at the Royal Naval College, with half the naval cadets and college staff suffering from the flu. So lethal was the infective virus, Mr J. Tucker a local Dock Union worker lost his wife and three children, all dying within a week.[23]

At Totnes 600 cases of influenza were reported with fifteen deaths, while at Okehampton over a 1000 of its population were infected and several deaths occurred.

At the end of November the influenza began to subside although thousands had suffered the loss of loved ones. Yet the dreadful experience of this viral disease, affecting so many people, has tended to obscure the serious outbreak of rabies that occurred in the West Country during 1918. A report in the *Western Mercury* states that fifteen cases of rabies had been confirmed in Plymouth and 140 dogs destroyed.[24]

Rabies is a neurotrophic virus lethal to man transmitted by infected dogs and certain other animals. A Board of Agriculture notice ordered that all dogs must be muzzled and a control placed on their movements. No dog was allowed to travel outside Devon or Cornwall. In Plymouth owners of unmuzzled dogs were prosecuted.

With all the trials and tribulations people were experiencing, 23 October was an especially sad day for many sailors from Devonport and Portsmouth. It was on this day that Dame Agnes Weston suddenly died at the Royal Sailors' Rest, Devonport. Born in London, daughter of a barrister, Dame Weston was

Two Devon nurses who were typical of the young women who found themselves called into service during the Great War. The hard work of such women and the comfort they provided to the wounded and sick earned them the highest respect. Sallie Cawsey (*seated*), A Red Cross nurse and Millicent Webber, trained at the North Devon Infirmary, Barnstaple.

known as the 'Blue Jacket's Mother'. Committed to her Temperance work, and keen to direct the young sailors away from the public houses, she encouraging them to sign 'the pledge', the reward being a cup of cocoa and a bun. At Devonport the 'Rest', better known to all as 'Aggie Weston's', and which started as a coffee bar and reading room, was throughout the war years a place of sanctuary and hospitality. Thousands of men including soldiers benefited from her charity and enterprise.[25]

1918 truly was the year of unexpected victory. The German Army had launched its massive offensive in the spring, overrunning the British and French lines on the Western Front. The Americans were beginning to deploy their forces although, as the American government was unwilling to integrate their army units with the Allied Command, they were assigned their own area of the Front.

Faced with these fresh troops, hampered by lengthening lines of supply and their troops exhausted, the German attacks petered out. In contrast the Allied and American forces began to advance, pushing back the Germans and breaking through the Hindenburg line. Although the Allies had not yet advanced into Germany the problems, particularly on the enemy's home front, caused Kaiser Wilhelm to abdicate and seek refuge in Holland, leaving the German politicians to sue for peace. The Armistice was agreed and signed in a railway carriage on 11 November 1918; fighting officially ceased at 11am on that date.

Expectations of an Allied victory had been speculated for some time based on war reports in the newspapers. In a village 10 miles from Exmouth the church bells had rung out weeks before the Armistice on a wild rumour that the war had ended.[26] Casper John, son of the famous artist and a fifteen-year-old cadet at Dartmouth Naval College, records that the officers and cadets were among the first people in England to hear that peace had been declared – the College having received the news direct by wireless from Portsmouth. John, who later became First Sea Lord, describes how 'we had the feed of our lives at a farm, huge rag in the evening, then a concert.' Casper John was later sent to continue his training on the Devonport Battleship HMS *Temeraire* that had served at Jutland.[27]

At Bideford news of the Armistice was brought to the town by airmen in a beflagged car driven from RAF Westward Ho! But the local people did not believe the news until they heard it from an official announcement made by the town's Mayor outside the Post Office in the High Street.[28]

A newspaper reporter on the *North Devon Herald* describes being in his Barnstaple office and, on hearing the voices of hundreds of people, there was no need to enquire the cause of the noise. Going out of his office into the street he felt he had been plunged into a sea of humanity, the crowds swaying to and fro to a rhythm like foam-created breakers as they swarmed around the newspaper office. Flags and bunting were already on display.

To hear about peace was not sufficient for some people who wanted to see the news in cold print, and this they did as an 'Official Peace' notice was placed in the newspaper office window. Barnstaple became a town of colour, red, white, blue and yellow (the latter colour to honour the Belgians), and it was a sight that would live on in the memory of thousands who flocked from surrounding country districts into Barnstaple.[29]

Not so very far away, at South Molton, the town crier made the formal announcement of the Armistice. Every window of the the town's shops,

offices and private residences exhibited the numerous telegrams that had been received.

The ringing of the bells at Holy Trinity church was the first that the population of Exmouth heard about the peace. The official notice was later displayed in the window of Crews & Sons. News quickly spread around the town and out to the country districts. Being a coastal town the street lighting had been subject to blackout but contrary to DORA the lights were now brilliantly lit. At very short notice the local churches and chapels held services of thanksgiving, with thousands attending and many more unable to gain admission. Celebrations and religious services continued throughout the week and a grand victory fete attracted a great crowd of people. To the delight of the onlookers six aeroplanes flew over Exmouth. Bonfires were lit and at Henrietta Place an effigy of the Kaiser was burnt.[30]

Similar celebrations were held at Teignmouth, signalled by the sounding of the steam laundry's siren. At Shaldon the immediate celebrations took the form of a religious procession. Notices were distributed asking all the residents to illuminate their windows to produced a blaze of light. The procession, headed by a cross bearer, proceeded to the entrance of the green where a wreath in memory of the fallen was placed. Alongside the euphoria people were aware of the grief felt by those who had lost a relative or friend during the war.

At Torquay the news of peace was received by wireless on board HMS *Onyx* anchored in Torbay. By 9.15am all the ships' sirens were sounding in the harbour. Airmen and Wrens appeared and marched along the Strand led by a bugler and the banging of a big bass drum. As the news spread church bells begun to peal, and soon every boat in Torbay was beflagged, as were all the town's shops. Even the horse-drawn vehicles and motor cars were decorated.

The Mayor of Torquay appeared on the balcony of the Queens Hotel to address the crowd but there was so much noise it was impossible for him to be heard. New Zealand troops stationed at St Marychurch were given leave until 11pm and they marched through the town to Haldon Pier, there to join in with the huge celebrating crowd.[31]

In Plymouth on 11 November 1918 the sky was dull and rain threatened. Just after 9am on this Monday morning there started some of the most remarkable scenes ever witnessed in the city. A cacophony of sound from ships' sirens and whistles, joined by the factories and warships, told the

Devonport Dockyard 1918 with ships decorated with flags in celebration of the war's end.

Front page of the *Western Morning News* the day after the signing of the Armistice. The crowd is pictured outside the newspaper's offices in Plymouth.

The Western Morning News.

Nº. 18,316. [REGISTERED FOR TRANSMISSION AS A NEWSPAPER IN THE UNITED KINGDOM]   PLYMOUTH, TUESDAY, NOVEMBER 12, 1918   PRICE 2ᴰ.

ANNOUNCING THE NEWS.

THUMBS UP! SCENE OUTSIDE THE OFFICES OF " THE WESTERN MORNING NEWS " IN PLYMOUTH YESTERDAY MORNING WHEN THE ANNOUNCEMENT WAS POSTED IN THE WINDOW THAT THE GERMANS HAD ACCEPTED THE ARMISTICE TERMS.

people of Plymouth that the war was over. The noise was so loud it could be heard in the village of Cornwood on the edge of Dartmoor. As Cornwood village school log records: 'shortly after assembly I heard the sirens and hooters of Plymouth sounding loud and prolonged blasts. I made the necessary preparations for hoisting the flag, as I anticipated that they signified the acceptance by the Germans of the Allied terms for the Armistice. It was not until 9.30am that I could obtain confirmation by telephone communication from Plymouth.'[32]

One nine-year-old Plymouth schoolboy, Bernard Crock, was on his way to school down College Road in Mutley, worried that he was late and wondering what form of punishment he would receive. Then he heard the howling and wailing of sirens and, arriving at school, found many of the pupils were going home. His anxiety was relieved when he received a pat on the back from a teacher and told 'there's no school today, go home as soon as you can.' Then as an afterthought the teacher told him 'put your cap on straight.' Returning home people were appearing at open windows, groups were gathering in the streets, and passing one shop he noticed someone had placed a flag among a group of cabbages. What he was observing was the start of a momentous day for Plymouth.[33]

Throughout the city celebrations continued. Although there had been no official announcement flags were hung from thousands of windows all through Plymouth, with huge flags draped from all the prominent buildings and strings of bunting hung across the roads. The hawkers were soon out doing a thriving trade selling rosettes.

Civilians and soldiers, mainly from the Devonshire Regiment, pose outside the Town Hall in Okehampton which has been decorated for the Armistice celebrations.

Church and school bells started to ring at intervals and continued for the rest of the day. Several thousand people congregated in George Street in the vicinity of the *Western Morning News* offices waiting for the official announcement to be published. The news finally came from the Admiralty at Mount Wise who telephoned the newspaper who at 11am placed the official notice in the window of their offices creating tremendous excitement.

The formal announcement was made by the Mayor of Plymouth in the Guildhall square. As the scenes of rejoicing were taking place, two lorries of German POWs passed by, coming to a halt because of the dense crowds. Even the prisoners looked pleased as they guessed what was happening, the crowd showing restraint towards their former foe.[34]

Beatrice Chase first heard about the Armistice from her servant she called 'Mr Bluejacket' who had been told by a child, who had in turn received the news from another child. To confirm this she sent her secretary to the Widecombe village Post Office to check if any telegrams had been received confirming peace had been declared. Being a Monday there was no other

At the war's end thousands of Colonial troops made their way home. Here Australian troops at Millbay dock, Plymouth, are waiting to embark on the hospital ship *Soudan*, 1918.

Boarding a tender at Millbay to be taken out to the SS *Bahia Castle*, July 1919, bound for Australia. Many of these people would have come to Britain to work in factories and to help with the war effort. Some are ex-servicemen, now back in civilian clothes.

way she could find out, other than by reading a newspaper, but these came by post and were always a day late.[35]

On the eve of the Armistice thousands of people had waited patiently in Exeter, milling between Bedford Square and Queen Square, expecting news of the final victory to be announced. As nothing was forthcoming on this Sunday night the crowd dispersed at 11pm. The following morning began with the usual street scenes of people and traffic, before news of the Armistice was received from Plymouth. At 10.50am a peace bulletin was placed in the window of the *Express & Echo* offices. Suddenly the High Street was transformed into a jubilant mass of people, cheering and waving flags. The office clerks left their stools, the workers their factories, and business establishments closed down for the day. Land Girls from the local farms downed tools and hurried into the city where the main streets were covered in confetti. Exeter City Silver Band stood on the Guildhall's portico playing music to the crowds below who took up the singing 'O God our help in ages past'. There was a great gathering at Exeter Cathedral with the Mayor leading civic officers to a solemn service arranged at short notice. The 3000 seats of the Cathedral were taken well before the service began and people stood packed in the aisles and sat round the pillars.[36]

Peace had at last come, but at a terrible price. Many wives were now widows, children fatherless, families bereft of sons killed. For many young women, having lost the man to whom they were betrothed, there would be no wedding. Quite literally, the war had taken away a generation of young men in Europe.

For many the fate of their loved ones would never be known and thousands who returned were blind, disfigured and mentally scarred. Their presence on the streets of Devon was a disturbing reminder of the horror of war for many years to come.

Others were to spend the rest of their lives with a chronic chest disorders, gassed on the Western Front. Shell shock and other mental traumas were life sentences of misery.

Peace celebrations at Ilfracombe 19 July 1919 with schoolchildren spelling out the word 'peace'.

Yet optimism was high, with hope for a better life for the men waiting to be demobbed. An indication of the total number of men in the armed forces is given in the following figures appearing in a census from the Drake Division of Plymouth in December 1918.[37] Rolls of Honour throughout Devon show similar figures.

Ward	Adults	Men away on Service
Mutley Ward	4379	964
Drake Ward	5988	1705
St Peters	6230	1297
Valletort	4793	1975
Mount Edgcumbe	3757	1767
Stoke	3681	1084
Pennycross	3295	1105
TOTAL	32753	9897 (30%)

HE whom this scroll commemorates was numbered among those who, at the call of King and Country, left all that was dear to them, endured hardness, faced danger, and finally passed out of the sight of men by the path of duty and self-sacrifice, giving up their own lives that others might live in freedom. Let those who come after see to it that his name be not forgotten.

Pte. Arthur John Short
Devonshire Regt.

The housewife was now allowed to make cakes and pastries using sugar and chocolate. The meat ration doubled for Christmas 1918, but it remained on ration until the following November. Butter and sugar continued to be rationed until 1920 and prices increased more than at any time since 1914.

The tedium of life continued, offset by the first Christmas of peace for five years. The traditional pantomime at the Theatre Royal, Plymouth, attracted crowds to enjoy 'Mother Hubbard', the program consisting of twelve scenes with a cast of over a 100 artistes.[38] The people who queued at the early door paid 6p, including war tax, for a seat in the gallery.

The warriors of the county were demobbed and returned home. Towns and villages welcomed them back with some form of reception and recognition of their service to their country. Plans were made for the construction of local war memorials and sacred lists to honour the men and women who had died and served. To this day these memorials bear witness to how the war decimated the male community.

Throughout Britain 6 July 1919 was designated 'Peace Sunday', an occasion for special services to be held in churches and chapels. The event was used for more formal thanksgiving, for example at Sheepstor every man who returned from the war was given £3, and one man who lost his leg received

£10. The wartime Parliament was dissolved on 25 November 1919, and a national election arranged for 14 December. During the hustings Mr Lloyd George, the outgoing Prime Minister, replied to his own question. 'What is our task?' He declared 'To make Britain a country fit for heroes to live in.'

Mr. and Mrs. T. Hooper, Raleigh-terrace, Exmouth, have the satisfaction of knowing that their three sons, officers in the British Army, are all in England. Each of them has served in the ranks, been over the top, and been wounded.

The Paris Peace Conference opened in January 1919 attended by delegates from 37 nations, but not until 28 June 1919 was the formal Peace Treaty signed in the Hall of Mirrors at the Palace of Versailles. Germany was to be punished and the treaty was too harsh for there to be an immediate hope of reconciliation. The 'Spoils of War' were shared out by the victorious major powers with frontiers of countries revised and the politics of Europe becoming so complicated that the interests of the peacemakers got lost in prolonged debates. Instead of concord there was discord among the victors and Field Marshall Foch prophetically remarked 'This is not peace, it is an Armistice for twenty years'. Indeed it was.

IN EVER LOVING MEMORY

OF

Arthur John

"JACK"

The beloved Son of John and Elizabeth Ann Short,

Who was killed in Action in France, Sept. 28th, 1918,

AGED 20 YEARS.

No loved one stood around him
To bid a fond farewell,
No word of comfort could he
Leave to those he loved so well.

We often think of days when
We were all together,
A shadow o'er our lives is cast,
One loved one gone for ever.

CHAPTER SIX REFERENCES

1 *The First World War* (1991), Malcolm Brown.
2 ADM 1 8518/ 51: Admiralty Secretary Papers. PRO.
3 *Royal Navy Aircraft: serials and units* (1992), R. Sturtivant and G. Page.
4 AIR 1 453/ 16/ 312/ 26: Marine Operation Stations of the RAF. PRO.
5 ADM 131 64: Station Records Plymouth. PRO.
6 AIR 1 645: Air History Branch Records. PRO.
7 *Western Morning News*, 28.9.1918.
8 Ref:1262 M/L112. DRO.
9 Ref:1262 M/L112. DRO.
10 *Western Morning News*, 3.8.1918.
11 *Exmouth Journal*, 17.12.1998.
12 Ref: 1262 M/ 112. DRO.
13 ADM 131 64: Station Records Plymouth. PRO.
14 *The Bloody Eleventh* Vol 3(1995), W.J.P. Aggett.
15 AIR 1 453/ 15/ 312/ 26: Marine Operation Stations of the RAF. PRO.
16 *Ilfracombe Chronicle*. 2.11.1918.
17 *North Devon Herald*. 26.9.1918.
18 *Under the Guns of the Red Baron* (1995), Norman Franks.
19 *Ilfracombe Chronicle*, 2.11.1918.
20 *Brixham Western Guardian*, October 1918.
21 Brixham Sanitary Authority Annual Report, 1918.
22 *Totnes Times*, 9.11.1918.
23 *Totnes Times*, 10.10.1918.
24 *Western Weekly Mercury*, 28.9.1918.
25 *Western Morning News*, 24.10.1918.
26 *Exmouth Chronicle*, 19.10. 1918.
27 *Casper John* (1987), Rebecca John.
28 *North Devon Herald*, 14.11.1918.
29 *North Devon Herald*, 14.11.1918.
30 *Teignmouth Gazette*, 13.11.1918.
31 *Torquay Directory*, 13.11.1918.
32 *The Book of Cornwood and Lutton* (1997), Cornwood Parish Project Group.
33 *Western Morning News*. 11.11.1918.
34 *Western Morning News*. 12.11.1918.
35 *Completed Tales of My Knights and Ladies.* (1919), Beatrice Chase'
36 *Express & Echo*, 11.11.1918.
37 *Western Independent*, 15.12.1918.
38 *Western Independent*, 15.12.1918.

ABBREVIATIONS
PRO   Public Record Office
DRO   Devon Record Office
WDRO West Devon Record Office
IWM   Imperial War Museum
DWI   Devon Women's Institute
DFHS   Devon Family History Society

Appendices

The following pages contain facsimiles of original documents relating to Devon during the period 1914–18 and are intended to supplement information provided in the main work.

APPENDIX A

Part of the official list of survivors following the sinking of the *Hogue* in September 1914.

SURVIVORS BELONGING TO H.M.S. " HOGUE "

O.N.	NAME	RATING	O.N.	NAME	RATING.
166855.	Thomas Cooper	C.P.O.	181978	Edward Thompson,	P.O.
190327	Henry Hughes,	P.O.	211561	Walter Lumby,	P.O.
186878	William T. Stewart,		156788	Andrew Finlayson,	M.A.A.
2994.R.F.R.	Jas J.Hughes,	P.O.	193544	Horatio Horrocks,	P.O.
188894	Fredk.E.Maxted,	P.O.	127948	Edward E.Grimerd,	Yeo.Sigs.
2493 R.F.R.	Wm.J.Kimp,	2 Yeo Sigs.	6132, R.F.R.	Fras H.Huntley,	Lg.Sig.
3779 R.F.R.	Geo J.Prior,	Ch.Sto.	41992, R.F.R.	Henry Tilley,	Ch.Sto.
306370	Mathew Hunter,	S.P.O.	345642	Tom Kay,	Elec.Art.
1217 R.F.R.	Wm H.Congdon,	M.A.A.	160076	Henry Snell,	S.P.O.
Pens.	Chas T.Noble,	Car Mte.	343930	Wm.Highfield,	Shpt.2cl.
Pens.	Jno.A.Tucker,	E.R.A.	158800	Wm.J.Tree, Dice	S.P.O.2.
11582 Pens.	Jas J.Padden,	S.P.O.	17886 Pens.	Stephen W.Stone,	E.R.A.
Chas. P.	Biglen. 768466	E.R.A.	4598	Isaac Girling.	A.B.
235965	Harry Page,	A.B.	B5319	Henry Bent,	A.B.
B4074	Fredk.Castell,	A.B.	B10121	Enock Kenyon,	A.B.
4770 R.N.R.	Walter Bicker,	A.B.	M1325	Albt.V.Tassell,	2 S.B.S.
B5297	Ed.J.Pike	A.B.	B5786	Geo.A Crouch,	A.B.
B3502 R.M	Saml Sprawson,	A.B.	2134 R.N.R.	Robert Weatherhead,	A.B.
J12684	Henry A.Ward,	A.B.	232199	William Blade,	A.B.
198142	Edward H.J.Canham,	A.B.	5119 R.N.R.	Wm.H.Dryden,	A.B.
10163 R.N.R.	Jas A.Hannan,	A.B.	1497	Ernest Wells,	Off.Std.2.
187080	Stephen L.Brooks,	A.B.	M2727 B.	Bernd.H.Culverwell,	Lg.Car.Cr.
B6641	Harry Gower,	A.B.	B10443	Thomas Berry Mc Donald,	A.B.
33564	William Eales,	A.B.Beatmn	B4297	Richd. F.Thornton.	A.B.
B819	Harry Langley,	A.B.	B10702	Thos. E.Goddard.	A.B.
B1219	Henry Symons.	Lg.Sig.	B8510	Willie Read.	A.B.
580 R.N.R.	Robert Gill		R.N.R.	Charles Green, 2253	L.S.
R.N.R.	Walter Welham,		10186 R.N.R.	Jos.H.Watts,	A.B.
199818	Alexr.P.Waldeck, RFR.	A.B.	B7169	Fredk.Clarke,	A.B.
J.26210	Geo.C.Styles.	Sig.Boy.	209443	Alfred Walden,	A.B.
7624	Jas H.Sidney,	Car Cr.	233818	Harry J.Moss.	A.B.
212079	Ern.Wm Wellard,	A.B.	217826	Geo.Spalding,	A.B.
4045 RFR	Geo.Huggins	A.B.	186281	Wm.Geo.Robinson,	A.B.
211013	Wm Cook,	A.B.	206211	Herbert Bullen,	Lg.Sea.
3029 RNR	John Beer,	A.B.	5126 RNR	John B.Peacock,	A.B.
245 RNR	C.C.Campbell,	A.B.	5185 RFR	Wm C.H.Bagley,	A.B.
6665 RFR	Richd J.Pett,	A.B.	B5321 RNR	Arth.G. Mc Cartney,	A.B.
4945 RNR	Wm.E.Cox,	A.B.	3572 RNR	Geo.A.V.Bailey,	A.B.
10568 RFR	Ernest Cannon,	A.B.	B10654 RFR	Leon.V.Moody.	A.B.
6637 RFR	Arthur Moore.	A.B.	B10667 RFR	Sidney D.Jones,	A.B.
195449	Richd.Marks.	Lg.Sea.	B10180 RFR	Richd.Wm. Demuth,	A.B.
6649 RFR	Wm Wakeley,	A.B.	A4258 RNR	David Featherby	A.B.
Fredk.F.Ferguson,	J6295	A.B.	B157170 RFR	Richd.Foggie.	A.B.
3032 RFR	Walter C.Wood,	A.B.	B3506 RFR	Wm H.Finch.	A.B.
222060	Chas Goody,	A.B.	M1687	Malcolm.Mc Millan,,	Cks Mte.
5712 RNR	Wm.H.Avery,	A.B.	347895	Walt.Wm. Hosker.	L.C.M.
6994.RFR	Arth Wm.Phillips.	A.B.	5310 B.	Geo.Edwards	A.B.
178095 RFR	Horace Lambert	A.B.		Frank G.Barker, 9387	A.B.
J	Jas.G.Chapman,	Lg.Sea.	R.F.R.B672	Robert Longmate,	A.B.
RFR B5785	Arthur Astell,	Sto.	177942	Chas A.Booth	P.O.
RFR B620	Samuel Formston.	A.B.	B 3042 RFR	Ernest Mills	A.B.

APPENDIX B
General Orders for Devonport issued 10 March 1915

DEVONPORT GENERAL ORDERS—Nos. 206—212.

202—205 Issued as "Confidential" General Orders.

206. **Correction to G.O. 201:** Line 1, *for* "N.E. ¾ W." *read* "N.E. ¾ N.".

207. Religious Ministrations in Gælic: A statement is to be forwarded, as soon as possible, showing the number of men of the Royal Naval Reserve, stationed at Devonport who belong to the Free Presbyterian Church, stating if possible the number who can speak Gælic.

C.E.20153, 6th March 1915. (No. 50/83.)

208. Plymouth—Precautions to be taken against aerial attack or bombardment (C.G.O. 178): The following proclamation issued by the Garrison Commander, Plymouth, is promulgated for information:—

Although an attack by enemy aircraft on, or a bombardment of, the towns of Plymouth and Devonport is *not* anticipated, still, it is considered advisable to be prepared for such, and instructions indicating the action which the public is advised to take in the event of an actual attack developing are, accordingly, published at the foot hereof.

Warning of any such impending attack will be made known in the following manner:
1. IN PLYMOUTH.

A series of *several short blasts* followed by *one long blast* from syrens or hooters at the works of certain local firms, at all hours of the day or night.

2. IN DEVONPORT.

(a) *By day.*—*Two guns at ten seconds interval* fired by *Impregnable*, and a red ensign hoisted at the foremast head. *Two guns fired by Naval Barracks at ten seconds interval.*

(b) *By night.*—*Two guns at ten seconds interval* fired both by *Impregnable* and *Naval Barracks.*

INSTRUCTIONS TO BE FOLLOWED IN THE EVENT OF BOMBARDMENT, OR ATTACK BY ENEMY AIRCRAFT.

1. The most important thing is to *keep calm and help others to do the same.*
2. Go to the cellar, or lowest room of your house, farthest away from the sea, and stand as far as possible from the glass. If you are out of doors seek the shelter of the most substantial building near you.
3. Do not rush into the street and never attempt to gather in crowds to see what is going on.
4. If there is any opportunity, turn off the gas at the meter. This might prevent fire. *Remember also (and this is of the greatest importance) subsequently to turn off the gas at the various burners.*
5. If you have to proceed through the town during the bombardment keep on the side of the street nearest to the sea, if such street runs parallel with the sea. Drivers of vehicles, especially heavy vehicles, may find it advisable to unyoke their horses in the streets in order to reduce the danger from alarmed horses. Drivers should, as far as practicable, proceed directly to their stables, or take up a sheltered position.
6. Unexploded bombs or shells should not be touched as they may burst if moved. The local military authority should be informed where they are.
7. In the case of bombs being dropped from aircraft, cellars are the refuges which afford the best chances of safety.
8. At night the most important precaution is to show no lights which would be visible from aircraft and enable them to identify towns and other places. Outside lighting should be reduced to a minimum.
9. If notice is received of the approach of aircraft, all outside lights of every description should be at once extinguished and kept extinguished for the rest of the night.

209. Trawlers have been allotted numbers and are to be regarded as having been commissioned as follows:—

Vessel		No. allotted	Date of commissioning	Vessel		No. allotted	Date of commissioning
Lord Allendale	... ...	1351	10 Feb. 1915.	*Ospray II*	... ...	1354	3 Mar. 1915.
Norse	... ...	1352	27 ,, ,,	*Oku*	... ...	1355	5 ,, ,,
Roche Castle	... ...	1353	2 Mar. ,,				

210. Closing of Bull Point Signal Station: From 1.0 p.m. on Saturday, 13th instant, until further orders, the signal station at Bull Point will be closed. *(No. 50/80.)*

211. Drafting of ratings suffering from venereal disease during the period of hostilities: Article 12, paragraph 4 of the Drafting Regulations is to be amended to read as follows:—

"Cases of simple uncomplicated Gonorrhœa are not to be drafted until all acute symptoms have "subsided. Any aggravated or complicated case is to be sent to hospital for special survey, "and for opinion as to whether the complication is grave enough or likely to be so prolonged "as to justify exemption from draft". *N.17822, 7th March 1915. (No. 50/88.)*

212. Mines are reported between N.E. Varne buoy and Colbart Ridge.

Naval Centre telegram, 8th March 1915.

ROYAL NAVAL COLLEGE,
DARTMOUTH,
24th March, 1916.   191

Sir,

In reply to A. L. No.M.39045 of the 12th instant
(Plymouth No.061) I have the honour to submit that the
following arrangements are in force in Dartmouth in the event of
a possible air raid;-

"On receipt of a preliminary telegraphic of telephonic
advice that enemy air craft have crossed the English Coast, the
Mayor of Dartmouth immediately instructs the Harbour Master to
stand by. On receipt of a second message to take action
(meaning that enemy air craft are travelling in the direction of
Dartmouth) the bells of St.Saviour's Church will be clanged
continuously for three minutes, as a signal to everyone in the
town to extinguish their lights. In addition to this signal the
Harbour Master will be instructed by the Mayor to instantly
extinguish the leading Harbour Lights, light at the Coast Guard
Station, also to order all lights on ships to be extinguished."

Notification will be given to this establishment by
the local Postmaster on the telephone, and the instructions set
forth in Memo. No.085A of 7th March,1916, will be followed.

I have the honour to be, Sir,

Your obedient Servant,

N. Palmer

Rear Admiral Commanding.

APPENDIX C
Instructions from the
Commander-in-Chief,
Devonport to the
Commanding Officer HMS
Britannia concerning air raid
precautions. March 1916.

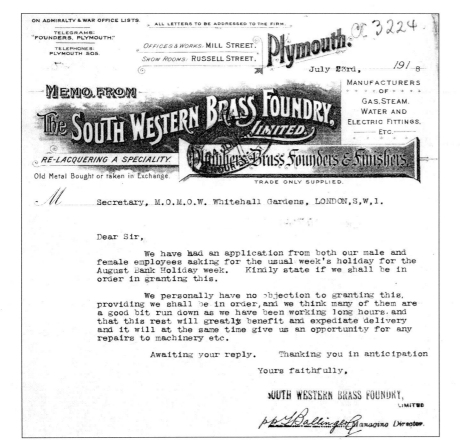

APPENDIX D
Commercial companies were
required to comply with the
Defence of the Realm Act
and other Government
orders requiring them to
seek permission to give
holidays to their workforce.

APPENDIX E

List of Devon
Territorial Units
serving abroad in
January 1917.

UNITS SERVING OVERSEAS,

1st JANUARY, 1917.

Unit.	New Title.	Date proceeded Overseas	Where Serving.
1/1st Royal 1st Devon Ymry.	16th Battn. Devonshire Regt.	Sept., 1915	Egypt.
1/1st Royal N. Devon Hussars	16th Battn. Devonshire Regt.	Sept., 1915	Egypt.
1/1st Devon Battery, R.F.A.	"A" Battery, 218th Brigade	Oct., 1914	India.
1/2nd Devon Battery, R.F.A.	"B" Battery, 218th Brigade	Oct., 1914	India.
1/3rd Devon Battery, R.F.A.	"C" Battery, 218th Brigade	Oct., 1914	India.
2/1st Devon Battery, R.F.A.	"A" Battery, 228th Brigade	Dec., 1914	Aden.
2/2nd Devon Battery, R.F.A.	"B" Battery, 228th Brigade	Dec., 1914	India.
2/3rd Devon Battery, R.F.A.	"C" Battery, 228th Brigade	Dec., 1914	India.
Ammunition Column, R.F.A.	28th Div. Ammn. Col., R.F.A.	Dec., 1914	Salonika.
No. 1 Heavy Battery Devon R.G.A. No. 2 Heavy Battery, Devon R.G.A.	159th (Devon) Heavy Battery, R.G.A.	June, 1916	France.
Devon Royal Garrison Artillery	48th Siege Battery, R.G.A. (Section).	April, 1916	France.
	117th Siege Battery, R.G.A. (Section).	March, 1916	France.
	No. 55 Anti-Aircraft Section	August, 1916	Egypt.
	No. 56 Anti-Aircraft Section	Sept., 1916	France.
	No. 62 Anti-Aircraft Section	Oct., 1916	France.
1/1st Wessex Divl. Sig. Co. R.E.	27th Wessex Divl. Sig. Co. R.E.	Dec., 1914	Salonika.
1/1st Works Co. Devon (F) R.E.	No. 567 Army Troops Co. R.E.	Dec., 1914	France.
1/2nd ,, Co. Devon F) R.E.	No. 568 Army Troops Co. R.E.	Oct., 1914	Gibraltar. (1)
1/3rd ,, Co. Devon (F) R.E.	No. 569 Army Troops Co. R.E.	Oct., 1915	Egypt.
1/4th E.L. Co. Devon (F) R.E.	4th (E.L.) Co. Devon (F) R.E.	Mar., 1915	Gibraltar.
1/4th Battn. Devon Regt.	- - -	Oct., 1914	Mesopotamia.
2/4th Battn. Devon Regt.	- - -	Dec., 1914	India.
1/5th Battn. Devon Regt.	- - -	Oct., 1914	India, absorbed in Terr. (Devon) Infan. in India.
2/5th Battn. Devon Regt.	- - -	Sept., 1915	Egypt. (2)
1/6th Battn. Devon Regt.	- - -	Oct., 1914	Mesopotamia.
2/6th Battn. Devon Regt.	- - -	Dec., 1914	India.
1/1st Wessex Fld. Ambulance	24th Field Ambulance	Dec., 1914	France.
2/1st Wessex Fld. Ambulance	- - -	Dec., 1915	France.
1/2nd Wessex Fld. Ambulance	25th Field Ambulance	Dec., 1914	France.
1st Wessex Clearing Hospl.	1st Wessex Casualty Clearing Station	May, 1916	France.
1/1st Wessex Sanitary Section	- - -	Oct., 1916	Mesopotamia.
2/1st Wessex Sanitary Sect.	- - -	Oct., 1916	Mesopotamia.

(1) Returned to England, December, 1916.

(2) Absorbed in 1st Line Devon Battalions, T.F.

TORQUAY.

Marine Operations (Seaplane and Balloon) Station.

(a) **No. 239 Squadron.** (b) **Sub-station of No. 16 Balloon Base (Merifield).**

(S.W. Area ; No. 9 (Operations) Group, 72nd Wing.)

LOCATION.—England, Devonshire, in the town of Torquay (pop., 38,700).
Railway Station :—Torquay (L. & S.W. Rly.), 1 mile.
Road :—Good urban road to the site.

FUNCTION.—(a) Station for No. 239 Squadron, Headquarters and Flights Nos. 418 and 419 (Float Seaplane), for Anti-submarine Patrol duties.

(b) A sub-station of No. 16 Balloon Base (Merifield). There are 3 Dummy Balloons which are sent out with Trawlers.

This Squadron and Balloon Sub-station are under the control of the Commander-in-Chief, Devonport for Operations.

ESTABLISHMENT.

Personnel.	Seaplane Station.	Balloon Base.	Transport.	Seaplane Station.	Balloon Base.
Officers	29		Light Tender ..	1	
W.O.'s and N.C.O.'s above the rank of Corporal ..	11		Heavy Tender ..	1	
		Included in the Establishment of Merifield.	Motor Cycle ..	1	Included in the Establishment of Merifield.
Corporals	13		Sidecar	1	
Rank and File	103		Ford	1	
Women	17				
Women (Household) ..	17				
TOTAL (exclusive of Hostel Staff)	190		TOTAL ..	5	

Machines.—For Seaplane Station : Float Seaplanes.. .. 12
For Balloon Base : Small Balloons 4

TOTAL 16

LAND.—The land occupied by this station is about 4 acres on the harbour to the south of the town of Torquay. Its water frontage is about 150 yards on Beacon Quay, between South Pier and Haldon Pier. There are fair mooring facilities and the water in the neighbourhood of the station is smooth

TENURE POLICY.—Not on the list of permanent stations.

ACCOMMODATION.

Technical Buildings.					Map Reference.
4 Seaplane Sheds—each 60′×48′ ..	..	..	..		1
Balloon Shed, 105′×60′ ..	..	..	..		1
3 Canvas Hangars, 66′×66′..	..	..	..		—
Workshops—Engineers', 55′×30′	..	..	..		—
Carpenters', 60′×30′	..	..	..		—
Dope Shop, 40′×20′	..	..	..		—
Blacksmiths' Shop ..	..	..	..		—
Oil Store	..	..	..		—
Petrol Store ..	..	..	..		—
General Store ..	..	..	..		—
Offices and Guard Room ..	..	..	..		—
Armoury ..	..	..	..		—
Detonator Store ..	..	..	..		—
Ammunition Store	..	..	..		—
Derrick (on Haldon Pier) ..	..	..	..		—
Pigeon Loft ..	..	..	..		—

Regimental Buildings.—Personnel is billeted. There is a " Day Quarters " Room, for Officers, on the Station. Sea Lawn Hotel is taken over for Personnel.

No. 11, Beacon Terrace is adapted for Women's Hostel, and Coastguards' Boat House for Women's Mess Room.

STATE OF WORKS AND BUILDINGS.—On 26th October, 1918, the percentage of progress was as follows :—

Sheds	..	..	..	..	..	..	75
Technical Buildings ..	..	..	..	..	..	80
Regimental Buildings and Adaptations	..	..	..	100
Roads, Water Supply and Drainage	..	..	..	100
Lighting ..	..	..	..	..	..	..	5

The estimated date of completion for the whole station is 31st October, 1918.

CATTEWATER (PLYMOUTH).

Marine Operations (Seaplane) Station, Nos. 237 and 238 Squadrons

(S.W. Area ; No. 9 (Operations) Group, 72nd Wing).

LOCATION.—England, Devonshire, ¼ mile south-east of Plymouth, on the shores of Plymouth Sound.

Railway Stations :—Turnchapel (L. & S.W. Rly.), ¾ mile. Plymouth (L. & S.W. Rly.), 6 miles by road. Usual access by ferry or motor boat from Plymouth.

Road :—The roads are bad owing to steep hills.

Name :—This station is sometimes called " Mount Batten."

FUNCTION.—(a) Station for No. 237 Squadron, Headquarters and Nos. 420, 421, 422 and 423 (Float Seaplane) Flights for Anti-submarine Patrol duties. No. 238 Squadron, Headquarters and Nos. 347, 348 and 349 (Boat Seaplane, F. 3 type) for Anti-submarine Patrol duties. These Squadrons are under the control of the C.-in-C., Devonport, for Operations.

(b) This station is also used as a Store Base and Repair Depôt (Seaplanes) for No. 9 (Operations) Group.

ESTABLISHMENT.

Personnel.		Transport.	
Officers	84	Touring Cars	1
W.O.'s and N.C.O.'s above		Light Tenders	2
the rank of Corporal ..	34	Heavy Tenders	3
Corporals	32	Motor Cycles	5
Rank and File	348	Sidecars	3
Women	50	Ford	2
Women (Household) ..	35	Trailers	1
TOTAL (exclusive of Hostel Staff)	583	TOTAL	17

Machines.—Boat Seaplanes (F. 3 type) 9
Float Seaplanes 24
TOTAL 33

LAND.—The area occupied by this station is 30 acres, on a small peninsula almost surrounded by Plymouth Harbour. It is ½ mile by boat from Plymouth. The water is sheltered, with good mooring facilities. It stands about 15 feet above sea level.

TENURE POLICY.—Not at present on the list of permanent stations.

ACCOMMODATION.

Technical Buildings.	Map Reference.	Regimental Buildings.	Map Reference.
4 Seaplane Sheds—		Officers' Mess	3
Two, 200′ × 100′ ..	1	5 Officers' Quarters	—
Two, 180′ × 60′ ..	1	Officers' Baths	—
3 Slipways	—	Officers' Latrines	—
2 M.T. Sheds..	—	Sergeants' Mess (used as	
Workshops—		Women's Quarters) ..	—
Engineers', 123′ × 20′ (in		Sergeants' Latrines ..	—
annexe)	—	Sergeants' Baths	—
Carpenters', 80′ × 33′ ..	—	Regimental Institute ..	4
Dope, 40′ × 20′ (in		Regimental Store	—
annexe)	—	6 Men's Huts..	—
Smiths' Shop	—	Men's Baths	—
4 General Stores	—	Men's Latrines and Ablu-	
3 Oil Stores	—	tion	—

General Haig's Special Orders of the Day concerning the 2nd Battalion Devonshire Regiment
following the action at Bois des Buttes

SPECIAL ORDER OF THE DAY
By FIELD-MARSHAL SIR DOUGLAS HAIG
K.T., G.C.B., G.C.V.O., K.C.I.E
Commander-in-Chief, British Armies in France.

The following citations which appeared in the Orders of the Day, No. 371, of the 5th French Army, on August 20th, 1918, on behalf of 2nd Battalion Devonshire Regiment, and 1/4th Battalion King's Shropshire Light Infantry, are published for the information of all ranks :—

(Translation.)

2ND BATTALION DEVONSHIRE REGIMENT.

On the 27th May, 1918, at a time when the British trenches were being subjected to fierce attacks, the 2nd Battalion the Devonshire Regiment repelled successive enemy assaults with gallantry and determination, and maintained an unbroken front till a late hour. The staunchness of this Battalion permitted defences south of A——— to be organized and their occupation by reinforcements to be completed.

Inspired by the sangfroid of their gallant Commander, in the face of an intense bombardment, the few survivors of the Battalion, though isolated and without hope of assistance, held on to their trenches north of the river and fought to the last with an unhesitating obedience to orders.

Thus the whole Battalion—Colonel, 28 Officers, and 552 Non-Commissioned Officers and men—responded with one accord and offered their lives in ungrudging sacrifice to the sacred cause of the Allies.

1/4TH BATTALION KING'S SHROPSHIRE LIGHT INFANTRY.

On the 6th June, 1918, when the right flank of a British Brigade was being seriously threatened by the progress of a heavy enemy attack, the 1/4th Battalion of the King's Shropshire Light Infantry, which had been held in reserve, was called upon to counter-attack an important position from which their comrades had just been ejected.

With magnificent dash this Battalion rushed the hill on which the enemy had established themselves, inflicting heavy losses on them, and in the course of hand-to-hand fighting captured an officer and 28 other ranks.

Thanks to this gallant and spirited recapture of the key to the whole defensive position the line was completely restored.

The dash, energy, and intrepidity with which, on this memorable occasion, the 1/4th Battalion King's Shropshire Light Infantry carried all before it was largely responsible for the retrieval of a situation which had temporarily become critical.

BERTHELOT,
General Commanding Fifth Army.

General Headquarters,

September 26th, 1918.

PRINTED IN FRANCE BY ARMY PRINTING AND STATIONERY SERVICES

Commander-in-Chief,
British Armies in France.

PRESS A—9/18

153

Official HMSO poster encouraging the public to familiarise themselves with the characteristics of friendly and enemy aircraft. What practical use this might have had in reality is left to the imagination.

APPENDIX J

Copy of an official plan of Okehampton military camp c.1919. It shows the separate stabling for the horses of officers and other ranks, and the barrack used by the permanent troops. Temporary accommodation was provided in bell tents. The railways siding serving the camp was about a mile distant.

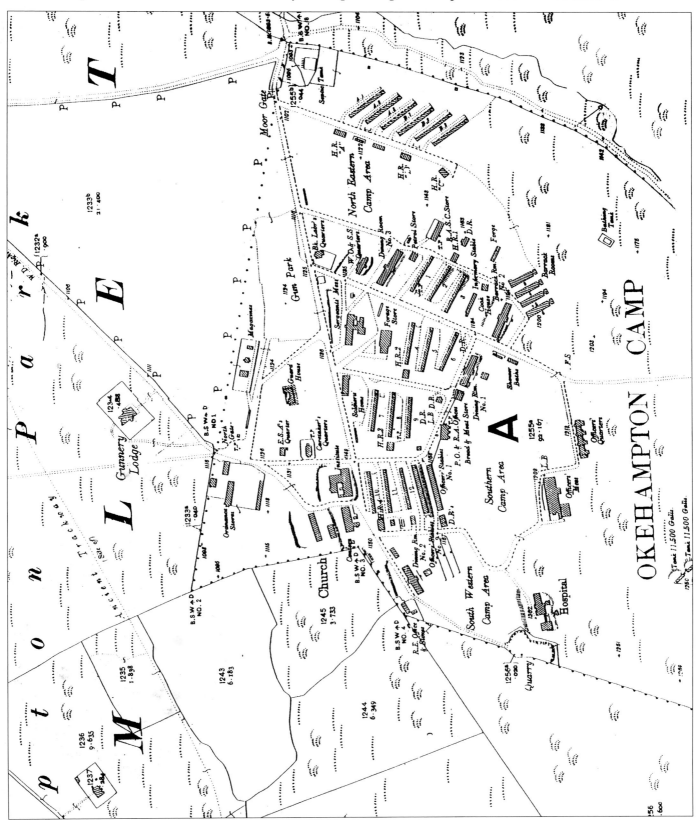

APPENDIX K

Royal Navy Dreadnoughts and destroyers tied up at Devon Dockyard at the end of the war.

Bibliography

Aggett, W.J.P. *The Bloody Eleventh* Vol. 2, 1994.

Aggett, W.J.P. *The Bloody Eleventh*, Vol. 3, 1995.

Aimer, Florence. *Mid Devon Early 20th Century*, 1992. Devon Family History Society.

Baldwin, Jean et al. *The Book of Manaton*. Halsgrove, 1999.

Bet-El, Ilana, R. *Conscripts: Lost Legions of the Great War*. Sutton, 1999.

Birdwood Field Marshal. *Khaki and Gown*. Ward Lock, 1941.

Brett, Dalla R. *History of British Aviation*, Vol. 2. Aviation Book Club, nd.

Bridgeland, Tony. *Sea Killers in Disguise, Q Ships and Decoy Raiders*. Leo Cooper 1999.

Brighouse, Ursula W. *Woodbury*. Privately published 1998.

Brown, Malcolm. *The First World War*. Sidgwick and Jackson, 1991.

Bruce, J.M. *Airco DH9*. Windsock Datafile (2), 1998.

Burkhalter, Paul. *Devonport Dockyard Railway*. Twelve Heads Press, 1996.

Brisco, Robert. *A Hundred Years of Co-operative in Plymouth*. Co-operative Press 1960.

Campbell Gordon, Vice Admiral. *My Mystery Ships*. Hodder & Stoughton, 1937.

Carson, Ritchie. *Q Ships*. Terence Dalton, 1985.

Chase, Beatrice. *Completed Tales of My Knights and Ladies*. Longman, 1919.

Chase, Beatrice. *The Dartmoor Window Again*. Longman, 1921.

Christie, Peter. *North Devon History*. Edward Gaskell, 1995.

Collier, Basil. *The Defence of the United Kingdom*. HMSO, 1952.

Costello, John. *Jutland 1916*. Weidenfield & Nicolson, 1976.

Crane, Harvey. *A History of the Theatre in the West Country*. Macdonald & Evans, 1980.

Davis, Mick. *Sopwith Aircraft*. Crownwood Press, 1999.

Delderfield, Eric R. *Exmouth Milestones*. Raleigh Press, 1948.

Delderfield, Eric R. *Cavalcade by Candlelight*. Raleigh Press, 1956.

Dicker, George. *A Short History of Devonport Royal Dockyard*. Private published, nd.

Dickinson, M.G. *A Living from the Sea*. Devon Books, 1987.

Dobinson, M. et al. *The Book of Cornwood and Lutton*. Devon Books, 1997.

Drury, R.W. Lieut Col. *In Many Parts*. Fisher Unwin, 1926.

Dudley, Ernest. *The Gilded Lily*. Oldham Press, 1958.

Duffy, Michael et al. *The New Maritime History of Devon*. Conway Maritime Press, 1994.

Duguid, A.F. *Official History of the Canadian Forces in the Great War 1914-1918*. Ottowa, 1938.

Dupre, Catherine. *John Galsworthy*. Collins, 1976.

Everitt, Don. *K Boats*. Airlife, 1999.

Fayle. *Seaborne Trade* Vol 2. Submarine Campaign. Official History, 1923.

Franks, Norman. *Under the Guns of the Red Baron*. Grub Street, 1995.

Freeman, Ray. *Dartmouth and its Neighbours*. Phillmore, 1990.

Freeman, Ray. *History of the Castle Hotel Dartmouth*. Dartmouth History Research Group, 1995.

Gaydon, Tina. *Braunton*. Badger Books, 1989.

Gibson, Mary. *Warneford VC*. Friends of the Fleet Air Arm Museum, 1979.

Gilbert, Martin. *Atlas of the First World War*. Routledge, 1994.

Goodman, Syd & Ballantyne I. *Plymouth Warships 1900-1950*. Halsgrove, 1998.

Gould, R.W. *Epic Actions of the First World War*. Tom Donovan, 1997.

Hall-Compton, Richard. *Submarines at Sea 1914-1918*. Macmillan, 1991.

Hames-Hayter, Jane. *A History of Chagford*. Phillimore, 1981.

Hardy, Florence Emily. *The Life of Thomas Hardy*. Macmillan, 1962.

Hart-Liddell. *A History of the World War 1914-1918*. Faber & Faber, 1936.

Hathaway, Sibyl. *Dame of Sark*. Heinemann, 1961.

Haythornthwaite, Philip J. *Gallipoli 1915*. Osprey, 1991.

Haythornthwaite, Philip J. *The World War One Source Book.* Arms & Armour, 1997.
History of the Ministry of Munitions 12 Vols. London, 1921–2.
Hohne, Heine. *Carnaris.* Secker & Warburg, 1979.
Holt, Valman and Tonie. *Violets from Overseas.* Leo Cooper, 1996.
Hornsey, Brian. *Ninety years of Cinema, Plymouth.* Privately published 1994.
Horseman, Grace. *Growing up between 1900-1920.* Cottage Publishing, 1996.
Humphries, Stephen. *Hooligans or Rebels.* Blackwell, 1981.
Huntford Roland. *Scott and Amundsen.* Hodder & Stoughton, 1979.
John, Rebecca. *Casper John.* Collins, 1987.
Jones, H. A. *The War in the Air, Vol 2 and 3. Official History of the War*, HMSO.
Keane, W.G. *Dartmouth College Hospital.* Dartmouth History Research Group.
Kingaby, G. *The Book of Morchard Bishop.* Halsgrove, 1999.
Kittridge, Alan. Plymouth. *Ocean Liner Port of Call.* Twelveheads Press, 1993.
Kolata, Gina. FLU. Macmillan, 2000.
Lee, Arthur Gould. *The Flying Cathedral.* Methuen, 1965.
Liddle, Peter H. *The Sailors' War 1914–1918.* Constable, 1972.
Lloyd George, D. *War Memoirs,* Vol 1–6. London, 1933-6.
London, Peter. *Aviation in Cornwall.* Air Britain Publications, 1997.
MacDonald, Pat. *Devon Within Living Memory.* Countryside Books, 1993.
MacPherson, W.G. Major General.
    Medical Services, Diseases of the War.
    History of the Great War. Vol. 1. HMSO, 1922.
Marwick, Arthur. *The Deluge.* Macmillan, 1979.
May, Arthur. *The True Glory. The Royal Navy 1914-1939.* Hodder & Stoughton, 1996.
Moor, William. *Gas Attack.* Leo Cooper, 1987.
Morgan, Jane. *Agatha Christie.* Collins, 1984.
Mowthorpe, CES. *Battlebags.* Sutton, 1998.
Murphy, Robert. *The British Cinema Book.* BFI, 1997.
Musolf, Karen J. *From Plymouth to Parliament.* Macmillan, 1999.
Newton, Robert. *Victorian Exeter.* Leicester University Press, 1968.
O'Brien, Terence H. *Civil Defence.* HMSO, 1995.
Oliver, Frederick Scott. *Ordeal by Battle.* Macmillan, 1915.
Pike, John. *Torquay the Place and the People.* Torquay Centenary Committee, 1992.
Pitt, Chris. *A Long Time Gone.* Portway Press, 1996.
Richards, R.G. *Through the Mists of Memory.* Privately published, 1995.
Richardson, R. *Through War to Peace 1914–1918.* Privately published, 1919.
Rowe, John. *The North Devon Yeomanry.* North Devon Museum, nd.
Royle, Trevor. *The Kitchener Enigma.* Michael Joseph, 1985.
Ryall, David H. *Lest We Forget: War Memorials Around South Molton.* South Molton
    Archive, 1993.
Saunders, Keith A. *Devon Aerodromes.* Sutton, 1994.
Scott, Reg. *Plymouth People 1907–1982,* Plymouth Guild of Community Service,
    1982.
Seward, Caroline. *The Book of Bampton.* Halsgrove, 1998.
Snelling, Stephen. *Passchendale 1917.* Sutton, 1998.
Stanbrook, Mary. *Old Dartmoor Schools Remembered.* Forest Publishing, 1991.
Stephen, Patrick. *British Vessels Lost at Sea 1914-1918.* Patrick Stephen, 1988.
Strachen, H. *First World War.* Oxford University Press, 1998.
Steel, Nigel & Hart, Peter. *Tumult in the Clouds.* Hodder & Stoughton, 1997.
Stevenson, John. *British Society 1914–1945.* Penguin, 1984.
Sturtivant, Ray & Page, Gordon. *Royal Navy Aircraft : serials and units 1911–1919.* Air
    Britain Publication, 1992.
Tall, J. J. & and Kemp, Paul. *HM Submarines in Camera 1903-1039.* Sutton, 1996.
Teague, Dennis C. *Mount Batten: Flying boat Base, Plymouth 1913-1986.* Westway
    Publications, 1986.
Thomas, David A. *Battle and Honours of the Royal Navy.* Leo Cooper, 1998.
Waller, Percy B. *Early Aviation at Farnborough.* MacDonald, 1971.
Walling, J. A. R. *The Story of Plymouth.* Westaway Books, 1950.
Williamson, Anne. *Henry Williamson.* Sutton, 1995.
Winter, J.M. *The Great War and the British People.* Macmillan, 1986.
Woodcock, G. *Tavistock's Yesterdays 5.* Privately published, 1989.
Zeigler, Philip. *Mountbatten.* Collins, 1985.

Index